CAPTURING OUR STORIES

CAPTURING OUR STORIES

An Oral History of Librarianship in Transition

A. ARRO SMITH
Foreword by Loriene Roy

Neal-Schuman
An imprint of the American Library Association
CHICAGO | 2017

ARRO SMITH, technical services manager at the San Marcos (Texas) Public Library, has been a practicing librarian for more than twenty-five years. Dr. Smith earned a master's degree in Library and Information Science and a PhD in Information Studies from the University of Texas at Austin. He is the author of numerous journal articles and book chapters, including the widely read "Cataloging Heresy," an essay that appeared in *Radical Cataloging* by K. R. Roberto (2008). Dr. Smith worked with former ALA president Dr. Loriene Roy, in a partnership between the American Library Association and the School of Information at the University of Texas, to create a national oral history program for retired and retiring librarians.

ISBN: 978-0-8389-1461-8 (paper)

Library of Congress Cataloging-in-Publication Data

Names: Smith, A. Arro, author.
Title: Capturing our stories : an oral history of librarianship in transition / by A. Arro Smith.
Description: Chicago : ALA Editions, an imprint of the American Library Association, 2017. | Includes bibliographical references and index.
Identifiers: LCCN 2016027171 | ISBN 9780838914618 (pbk. : alk. paper)
Subjects: LCSH: Librarians—United States—Biography. | Capturing Our Stories Oral History Program of Retiring/Retired Librarians. | Librarians—Interviews. | Librarians—Attitudes. | Librarians—Effect of technological innovations on. | Retirees—Interviews. | Library science—United States—History—20th century. | Libraries—United States—History—20th century. | Collective memory. | Oral history.
Classification: LCC Z720.A4 S65 2016 | DDC 020.92/2 [B] —dc23 LC record available at https://lccn.loc.gov/2016027171

Cover photograph (top) © David Rees/Environmental Protection Agency, Librarian at the card files at a senior high school in New Ulm, Minnesota, 1974. Photos (below and right) © Shutterstock, Inc. Book design by Kim Thornton in the Freight Text, Freight Sans, and King typefaces.

♾ This paper meets the requirements of ANSI/NISO Z39.48–1992 (Permanence of Paper).

Printed in the United States of America

21 20 19 18 17 5 4 3 2 1

Contents

Foreword

BY LORIENE ROY, PHD

HOW APPROPRIATE TO START WITH A MEMOIR IN A FOREWORD TO A book of oral histories!

Each year one fortunate person serves as the president of the American Library Association (ALA). After being selected president-elect in 2006, I held the position of president during 2007–2008. People still ask me what that experience was like, and in many ways I am still regaining my energies from that intensive and exciting time. In short, I had to attend to three categories of tasks during my time as ALA president. One category was the work required of each ALA president, such as chairing meetings of the ALA Executive Board, ALA Executive Council, and ALA Council; completing media interviews; arranging for the ALA President's Programs; and preparing the President's Message for *American Libraries.* The second category of work involved responding to the issues that arose. In my case these issues included sharing the message that public libraries could help the public prepare for the transition to digital television and responding to censorship cases, such as the elimination of *abortion* as a search term in MEDLINE and the removal of copies of Philip Pullman's book *The Golden Compass* from library collections. The third category of tasks related to any initiative the ALA president wants to continue or launch, options that have become increasingly streamlined during the terms of more recent

ALA presidents. The initiatives I explored focused on recognizing library services as well as the contributions of individual librarians.

One example of how I was able to recognize the efforts of libraries reflected my interest in international librarianship. As ALA president-elect and ALA president, I had the good fortune to travel, completing fifty-two trips during my presidential year. Of course, ALA is concerned with libraries, and that travel brought me to libraries in Aotearoa (New Zealand), China, Mexico, South Africa, Canada, Australia, and many locations in the United States. This travel inspired me to launch a way to recognize outstanding library services and initiatives across the globe through the awarding of the ALA Presidential Citation for Innovative International Library Projects. Citation recipients are now selected by a committee of the International Relations Round Table and are recognized annually at the International Reception held at the ALA Annual Conference.

Although ALA's concentration is on the library and librarians, the emergence of its companion organization, the ALA Allied Professional Association (ALA-APA), renews a focus on the library worker. ALA-APA reminds us of the contributions of the individual and confirms that those working in libraries also need support and recognition whether through a certification process, information on salaries, or information about pay equity or unions. Attention to the retired librarian also is seen in the recent formation of the Retired Members Round Table (RMRT) of ALA.

Work in libraries is about the individual patron and library worker. As a professor, my work is also centered on the individual—students, clients with whom we collaborate, and alumni and potential employers. When I first became ALA president-elect, a friend, Tim Ditlow, told me that people from my past would return to my life. And he was right. Five hundred people danced in front of, beside, and behind me at the Honor Dance that the National Museum of the American Indian hosted for me in June 2007. Four days later, 520 people attended my inaugural banquet, including two of my sisters, friends from Aotearoa (New Zealand), my son Owen Hunter and his classical guitar octet Bella Corda, and the best cover band in Austin, the Eggmen. A few months later, my high school Spanish teacher met me at the bottom of the escalator to baggage claim at Duluth International Airport, holding up the cover page of the Duluth *News Tribune,* featuring an article that announced my return to my homeland: "Big Reader Leads County's Big Read." As I spoke from podiums in locations ranging from Cloquet, Minnesota, to Denver, Oklahoma City, Tulsa, Louisville, Las Cruces, and Portland, Oregon, I looked out on crowds that often included a former teaching assistant, a former student, or my own high school teachers or professors from the University of Arizona or the University of Illinois at Urbana-Champaign. And though the events provided me the opportunity to share news about ALA, summarize my own work, or address a conference topic, it was the opportunity to hear the unique stories of the everyday lives of librarians that most resonated with me.

As I heard about impending retirements of librarians known for their professional contributions, I grew concerned about the lack of a conduit by which their life lessons could be gathered. I had worked on several previous oral history projects—documenting thematic interviews of the lower Colorado River region, helping design a program for the Association for Library Service to Children, helping coordinate oral history interviews for the Texas Library Association. I knew of the work of Dr. Martha Norkunas and witnessed the way her courses on oral history influenced how students in our School of Information approached their research. I felt that librarians, too, would have extensive stories to share. These would be the stories of decisions that led to educational paths and career choices. These would be stories of details, of response in the midst of a changing profession, all tempered by the emotional impact of regret, opportunity, and life history review. As a fan of StoryCorps, I even entertained the presence of a mobile technology lab enabling interviewees and interviewers to gather and share.

But, as my friend Beth Hallmark often reminded me, ideas are a dime a dozen. To bring an idea to fruition takes the commitment of one person. In this case, Arro Smith, always responsible and personable, dedicated years of reading, writing, and coordinating, leading to the capture of thirty-five professional life histories and their interpretation.

I invite you to read the stories of your colleagues and friends. Their stories are yours as well. I also invite you to consider extending *Capturing Our Stories* and participating in the legacy of librarianship by sharing your knowledge and experiences with your younger peers within your own library and by interviewing others. Please do this before you regret not having done so.

Acknowledgments

THE AUTHOR GRATEFULLY ACKNOWLEDGES THE FOLLOWING INDIVIDUALS who made this work possible:

Dr. Loriene Roy, who inspired my career as a public librarian when I was in library school (the first time), who encouraged my doctoral work many years later, and whose vision created the *Capturing Our Stories* project that forms the basis of this book.

David Gentry, my husband, who humored and fed me through my doctoral studies—and built an office in our backyard so my dissertation could be completed. And then continued to humor and feed me while I rewrote the dissertation to become this book.

Stephanie Langenkamp, my boss, counsel, and friend who very patiently showed me how to be an effective librarian and a true public servant. And the staff of the San Marcos Public Library who have supported and indulged me during this research work.

Dr. Martha Norkunas, the woman who taught me how to listen—and how to use oral history methodology to document our stories.

Dr. Ruramisai Charumbira, who patiently taught me how to be a historian—and how to use memory studies theory to hear what our stories had to say.

Margaret Ann Smith, my mother, who transcribed many, many hours of oral history interviews for this project.

Preface

MY STORY

MY DEAR FRIEND, COLLEAGUE, AND ADVISOR LORIENE ROY BEGAN THIS collection of stories with her story in the foreword. Now I'll tell you some of my story.

My library career began in 1990 when I graduated from the Graduate School of Library and Information Science at the University of Texas at Austin. I was one of Dr. Roy's first students at the beginning of her career as a professor. She inspired me to become a public librarian, and I have worked at the San Marcos (Texas) Public Library my entire professional career. I am a cataloger.

Dr. Roy and I stayed in touch after I completed my MLIS, and I always enjoyed sitting with her at the alumni suppers held during the Texas Library Association Annual Conference. It was at one of these conference suppers that the dean of the Texas school, now known as the School of Information, implored the practicing librarians present to consider returning to school for a doctorate so that we could teach. He mentioned many of the prevailing statistics about the "graying" of the profession and the fact that many of his faculty were quickly becoming *emeriti.* Dr. Roy gently kicked me under the table and whispered, "You." I took up Dr. Roy's challenge, and she served as my committee chair for the dissertation on which this book is based.

This notion of the "graying of the profession" is well documented in the library literature, beginning in the late 1990s and continuing through the next decade.[1] A sea change in library personnel occurred at the beginning of the millennium because so many professionals had entered the library workforce in the late 1960s and early 1970s.

But back to my story. To tell you the truth, I was not even interested in oral history. I was going to do my dissertation using quantitative research methods to examine subject-heading and authority records (I am a cataloger, after all). But the University of Texas insists that all its doctoral students study both quantitative and qualitative research methods as part of their plenary curricula. To satisfy this requirement I happened to be taking a class in the Anthropology Department that introduced me to oral history methodology. And Dr. Roy happened to be ALA president-elect.

When you are ALA president-elect, you may organize some special projects for your tenure as ALA president. One of Dr. Roy's Presidential Initiatives was to document the collective wisdom of this generation of librarians who were quickly retiring—and dying. I was not interested in this project, but when you are ALA president-elect, your Midwinter and Annual Conference schedules are packed with meetings and obligations. When you are ALA president-elect, you bring flunkies, friends, and people who owe you favors to Conference so that they can attend the meetings that you cannot. As Dr. Roy's doctoral student, I was her flunky. And this flunky was sent to a meeting about a nascent oral history project to document the professional lives of retiring and retired librarians.

And, frankly, that meeting was awful. There were many great ideas about how to do this project, but no real leadership to make it happen. It also happened that my current dissertation topic was quickly going down in flames due to a change in personnel at the library school. As I was reporting on the meeting to Dr. Roy that afternoon, it occurred to me that I might be able to make this Presidential Initiative happen for her—and I might just be able to use this project to finish my PhD.

Later in this book, Dr. Billie Grace Herring will colorfully describe the time when the library school dean asked her to stay on and take an available scholarship for a doctorate: "You talk about a gift landing in your lap!"[2] That perfectly describes my own experience working with Loriene Roy on this project.

Dr. Roy gave me the opportunity to make her American Library Association Presidential Initiative a reality. "You talk about a gift landing in your lap!"

And along the way, I became a really good oral historian and cultural anthropologist. I came to fully embrace qualitative research methods, feminist theory, and the power of many voices to tell one story.

Capturing Our Stories: A National Oral History Program of Retired and Retiring Librarians is an American Library Association partnership with the School of Information at the University of Texas at Austin. *Capturing Our Stories* gathers professional histories of experienced librarians as they exit their careers and makes those histories accessible to colleagues, students, and less-experienced librarians using state-of-the-art digital archiving tools through the Internet. The website for the *Capturing Our Stories* project is hosted by the School of Information at the University of Texas at Austin. Please visit it at www.ischool.utexas.edu/~stories/ to listen to and watch the videos of most of the interviews. Transcripts, which are keyword searchable, scroll along synched with the interviews. Permanent copies of all the interviews are part of the American Library Association Archives at the University of Illinois at Urbana-Champaign. Both the recordings and the transcripts are available through Illinois's online catalog at www.archives.library.illinois.edu.

I worked with Dr. Roy and the American Library Association to organize a cohort of volunteers to interview librarians at the end of their careers. We used oral history methodology, which calls for the interviewer to simply prompt the subject to tell her story in her own way. (It is clearly different from journalism. There were no set questions. It was not a survey.) I conducted twelve of the interviews myself. Thirty-five interviews were collected in total.

At first we simply used voice recorders, which is the standard oral history method. But when word spread through the library school of Dr. Roy's project and my involvement, Quinn Stewart, the information technology guru at the School of Information, called us into a meeting to demonstrate a powerful new tool to combine video interviews with searchable transcripts and stream the results on the Internet. This rich-media technology, GLIFOS, had been developed by a colleague at the University of Texas, and it was available for our use. So we began using camcorders to video record the interviews.

Successful doctoral research involves doing something that no one else has done previously. It must be unique research that expands our knowledge. My project, under Dr. Roy's supervision, was unique in two respects. I used state-of-the-art streaming technology to present an oral history project to a wide audience. When you read a quote from a librarian in the stories that follow, please know that you may go to the *Capturing Our Stories* website or to the ALA Archives at the University of Illinois at Urbana-Champaign and listen to the audio recording for the individual's inflection—and in most of the interviews you may watch the librarian's expression—to see if you agree with my interpretation and transcription. It is all there. All my raw data is available for you—and future researchers—to study.

This preservation method (combining the recording with the searchable transcript and making it available on the Internet) was unique among oral histories at the time. The other unique aspect of my research that qualifies it as a successful doctoral study is the use of theory. Maurice Halbwachs posited that all our memories *are* our memories because we share them with at least one other living person. He believed memories *must* be collective to exist at all.[3] Oral historians have eyed this theory for many years, and Alessandro Portelli has employed these ideas in his research about specific memories shared in Italy,[4] but no one had interviewed a sizable sample of one population using oral history methodology to produce a collective memory of a profession using Halbwachs's theory. This is what I have done.

My successful dissertation is not an easy read. It includes an exhaustive literature review to document the ways my research is unique and to establish the relevancy of the research. It has a very long discussion about the methodology and theories involved. And it includes an attempt at historicism (don't ask). This book intends to be just the good stuff. (My editor has insisted.) Part 2 of this book provides a primer of the theories and methodology I used, as well as tips on how to conduct your own oral history project.

This is the story of librarianship in the last half of the twentieth century told by thirty-five individuals. I have collected these oral history interviews and "listened" to hear a collective story of the profession emerge. Each individual story is unique, but together the stories are often the same story told over and over. I listened for repeating themes. They are presented here to tell the story of librarianship in our own voices, in our own way. I hope you enjoy them.

NOTES

1. John Berry, "Problems of a 'Graying' Profession," *Library Journal* (1986), 6; L. Darby, "Abolishing Stereotypes: Recruitment and Retention of Minorities in the Library Profession," *Bookmobiles and Outreach Services* 7(2), (2004), 9–18; A. V. Level and J. Blair, "Holding On to Our Own: Factors Affecting the Recruitment and Retention of Science Librarians," *Science and Technology Libraries* 27(1/2), (2006), 185–202; P. A. Mosley, "Mentoring Gen X Managers: Tomorrow's Library Leadership Is Already Here," *Library Administration and Management* 19(4), (2005), 185–92; D. Zabel and C. Van Fleet, "An Interview with 2006–07 ALISE President Connie Van Fleet," *Reference and User Services Quarterly* 47(3), (2008), 204–6; R. T. Lenzini and C. Lipscomb, "The Graying of the Library Profession: A Survey of Our Professional Association and Their Responses," *Searcher* 10(7), (2002), 88; G. Arthur, "The 'Graying' of Librarianship: Implications for Academic Library Managers," *Journal of Academic Librarianship* 24(4), (1998), 323–27.

2. Billie Grace Herring, interview by Michael McCombs, October 21, 2011, video recording, transcript, A. Arro Smith "Capturing Our Stories" Oral Histories Program, 2005-2012 97/1/70, American Library Association Archives at the University of Illinois, Urbana-Champaign, 14:17.

3. Maurice Halbwachs, *On Collective Memory* (Chicago: University of Chicago Press, 1992); M. Halbwachs, *The Collective Memory* (New York: Harper and Row, 1980).

4. Alessandro Portelli, *The Death of Luigi Trastulli, and Other Stories: Form and Meaning in Oral History* (Albany: State University of New York Press, 1991); A. Portelli, *The Order Has Been Carried Out: History, Memory, and Meaning of a Nazi Massacre in Rome* (New York: Palgrave Macmillan, 2003).

Part I

CAPTURING OUR STORIES

I don't know if I should tell this one, but I will.
—Dr. Bill Mears

What else can I say? Talk to people. Talk to people. Please. Don't be shy. There's—I spent today—this has nothing to do really with what we were talking about. I sat down at a table today for lunch with a cataloger. I had never met her before—there was an empty place at a table—and I sat down. A little while later, another lady came along, and she sat over there, and we said, "Come on, come on, join us!" It turned out that she was a cataloger too—for the Library of Congress—and the two catalogers got into a discussion about personalities. And they decided they were both introverted and—I'm definitely not introverted—we started talking "Librarians: What are they? What aren't they?" We went the gamut from how non-conservative are most librarians—how liberal, how far to the left, how standing by the library rules and rights—all the way back to jokes that catalogers tell on one another. It was just hilarious; it just went on and on. And none of us wanted to stop. And this is typical activity. Never sit in a corner: just join a group and start talking. I think that is the best way to learn about where you want to be? Is that—?[1]

This passage is from Valerie Feinman's oral history interview for the *Capturing Our Stories* project. She is talking about her experience at the 2008 American Library Association Annual Conference in Anaheim, California. Valerie attended a preconference workshop I held for the project that year, was one of our first interviewees, and has been my chief cheerleader for the project's duration. Her enthusiasm for sharing stories shines through in this brief quote from her interview. This book is about these stories about librarianship that we share among ourselves.

Please sit down and join the conversation.

In my preface, I alluded to the theory that underscored my dissertation—that shaped it. The short version of that theory is that if we listen to many people tell their personal story about being a librarian, certain elements will be repeated—each time in a new voice and with different words—that represent the "social memory" of librarianship. This is the memory that this generation shares of what it was like to be a librarian. And because it comes from many voices telling their personal stories, it will be different from an encyclopedia article detailing the aspects of a career in librarianship. This social memory will include feelings and attitudes about the career that cannot be captured any other way.

This is a story about librarians telling the story of librarianship. Many voices have been recorded to form a story of librarianship that describes a generation of librarians who began their craft using what we would now call "analog" technology—typewriters and card indexes—and retired fully immersed in the digital age. These are the information professionals who ushered the technological age into existence. Their "library science" gave birth to "information science." They are the Mothers and Fathers of the Information Age.

This story about librarianship begins with the social memory of making the decision to become a librarian. Each is different, but a surprising number of interviewees had no intention of becoming a librarian. Many librarians began their careers as teachers. I call these "accidental librarians." The first chapter concludes with a memory we all share no matter what kind of librarianship we ultimately practice: library school. Many of these library school memories are about the difficulty of cataloging class. In fact, these cataloging class memories are so prevalent that the discussion becomes a library cliché. Chapter 2 looks deeper into the clichés and stereotypes within the profession and in popular culture.

This cohort of librarians remembers the ways "it used to be done" and was instrumental in the introduction of the computer and "the way it's done now." There is a nostalgic social memory of the typewriter and the card catalog. And there is pride that we introduced technology to the masses with our clunky, DOS-based OPACs—and then became "information scientists." The third chapter, on technology, includes both nostalgia and memories of innovation.

Because these are librarians at the end of their careers, they have a long view of the profession. Most have become "very successful" and have become administrative leaders within their organizations and institutions. A surprising detail emerges from the social memory of librarianship: many regret being promoted. Many long for their entry-level positions and the hands-on practice of librarianship. Many plan to return to that work as volunteers after retirement. The fourth chapter looks at not only these regrets but also issues of sexism and compensation. And the fifth chapter examines the most recurring trope across all the interviews: these librarians enjoyed a very rewarding career because they were helping people find the information and resources they needed.

The concluding chapter of part 1 attempts to sum up the collective memory of librarianship. The ultimate story of librarianship—the story told over and over—is that this profession was the right choice for these people because it let them do something that really mattered. They helped people. Over and over.

NOTE

1. Valerie Feinman, interview by Sarah Albert, June 29, 2008, video recording, transcript, A. Arro Smith "Capturing Our Stories" Oral Histories Program, 2005-2012 97/1/70, American Library Association Archives at the University of Illinois, Urbana-Champaign, 39:12.

Chapter 1

BECOMING A LIBRARIAN

LIBRARIANS SHARE MANY OF THE SAME STORIES. WE ALL contribute to a shared narrative—a shared story. And all of us have a story to tell about the decision to become a librarian, often after an encouraging librarian in our childhood led us to discover the wonders of the library. Let's begin this project by recounting our earliest memories of libraries and our decisions to become librarians. The reasons we have chosen this vocation are individual and many; however, many shared narratives will emerge. This chapter concludes with memories we all share: our time in library school earning the qualifications for our vocation.

The Decision to Become a Librarian

Two future librarians report setting out to read every book in their childhood libraries. Peggy Richwine attended a very small school with only four classrooms. The "library" consisted of shelves along the walls of the four rooms. She set a goal of reading all the books. "So I read every one of them. And I'd take one home every night and read it, and return it the next day, and take another one home the next day."[1]

Karen Breen reports starting from *A* and working through the collection at her high school library. Ms. Breen remembers her early childhood library sharing a building owned by her grandfather. His plumbing shop was in the other half. She spent many afternoons in the library as her grandfather worked next door.

> **I can remember reading all the time. I can remember pretending that I was completely engrossed in a book so that when my mother would call me, and I didn't answer, she'd say, "Oh, she's just reading."**
>
> **I didn't know what I was going to do when I was in high school. My mother did the typical "Well, you read all the time, why don't you become a librarian?" And it was like, you know, the clouds parted and the sun came out. And then when I realized that being a librarian meant that I was always going to learn things—that people would ask me questions and I would research with them so that I would continue to learn—I decided that I wanted to be a librarian. In library school I took a children's lit course and knew right then that's what I wanted to do.**[2]

Ms. Breen's later childhood involved a great deal of moving while her father was in the military. She remembers that the library—in whatever temporary city they were stationed—could always be counted on to provide emotional stability: "The library was the only place that I knew to get the things that made me the happiest. And that was books."[3]

Bill Mears tells two stories from his childhood. The first is his recollection of learning about the public library. He was already an avid reader before discovering the library, and he spent his money buying Hardy Boys books from the stationery shop in his neighborhood. They were ninety-nine cents each. He collected Coke bottles with a two-cent redemption value in order to fund his reading habit. He clearly remembers the astonishment he felt upon finding out that the public library would lend him Hardy Boys books for free—and that he could spend his Coke bottle money on the cinema, which only cost nine cents.

Dr. Mears's second childhood library memory continued to influence his library values throughout his long career:

> **And I think that I will always, always remember this—I can still see this scene in my mind: Being a young boy, and being interested in things, I one time—I kept looking in the library for books on a certain subject—I'll tell you it was sex. And I could never find this book, so—I didn't want to go up and ask at the desk—but after enough weeks of looking, I finally went up to the desk, and I asked this librarian that was at the desk, "Do you have such-and-such book?"—I can't remember the title. And with that, she started, "Why does a young man your age want to look at that type of book—?"**
>
> **And about that time, a nice woman from behind the scene came onto the scene and said, "Mary"—or whatever her name was—"I'll take care of this." And she came up to me, and she said, "We keep that book behind the desk. Do you think you are old enough to read this?" And I didn't know what to say, so I said, "Yes." And so she gave me that book, and I got to look at all the pictures in that book, and was contented and turned it back in.**
>
> **And I always to this day remember the kindness of that woman, because I was so embarrassed. And love that woman for that, and I still think of that woman kindly, and always insist that my staff treat people with respect—especially kids.**[4]

Dr. Mears's career has been expansive. He was the director of a large university library but has also led a public library, a seminary library, and a prison library.

> **I started off as a—kind of a—a forced volunteer at a junior high library. I was involved in a program, and the principal said, "When you are not doing anything in this program, go help out in the library." And that was my initial introduction to being involved in working in a library.**

> **After that, I went to library school, and [I] was very much involved from that point forward in libraries. I was the assistant director of public services at the University of Southern Mississippi. I was the director at a community library in Ohio.**
>
> **I came back and started off as the assistant director at Texas State University, formerly Southwest Texas State University. I was there for twenty-five years.**
>
> **After I retired I went to help someone out—they called me and asked me to help automate the Episcopal Theological Seminary while they were hiring a director—and it was only supposed to be for three months. Well, the search fell through, and I ended up being there for eight months—and I really enjoyed that stay in a seminary library.**
>
> **After that, I went to a prison library. I was the director of a men and women's prison library for two years. And then a friend of mine told me about the availability of a public library's director position in Kyle. And I took that position and I have been there ever since—and I really enjoy that.**[5]

Dr. Mears is detail oriented, as most good librarians are. During his tenure at Southwest Texas State University, he was able to build a new library for the campus. It is one of his most dear accomplishments. However, he does regret one thing about that process: the main book return at the circulation desk was engineered incorrectly so that no standard book drop cart can fit under the slide. The books must slide to the floor and a clerk must pick up each one. He specifically remembers going over this detail with the architects and carefully measuring to make sure it would all work ergonomically, but the measurements were taken before the granite flooring was installed—and the book truck has never fit correctly. It is a testament to his character that one of his greatest professional regrets is that a clerk must pick up the books from the floor.

Richard Corson tells of an early childhood crush on the librarian. He was already an avid reader, but the attractions of Miss Charlotte Moughton, who worked at the Winter Park, Florida, public library, helped spur his interest. Another crush on another librarian (student) led to marriage. Both Richard and his wife are librarians.

Richard's wife, Connie Corson, became interested in librarianship when she entered art school as an undergraduate:

> **It was kind of a decision by default. I was an art student of in-studio art and art history at Queens College before it was part of the City University, and the college had a wonderful art library. . . . And I right away decided that I wanted to work in that library as a student assistant, you know? . . . So I needed a job and found one in the art library where I worked for four years.**
>
> **And when it was time for me to graduate, I decided what am I going to do now, you know? Am I going to be able to sell paintings? Am I going to be able to make pottery? And so on. And I had a wonderful librarian there who was my mentor all those years. Stanley, Dr. Stanley Lewis was his name. And I went to him and I said, "Dr. Lewis, I don't know what to do. I am graduating." And he was a professor at the Columbia Library School and he taught art librarianship there and he said to me, "Why don't you become a librarian, become an art librarian?" And it was like a eureka moment, you know?**
>
> **What a great idea—that I could still continue to be in the field of art but as a, you know, with a library background. So I enrolled in Columbia and I had to work, so the next thing I asked Dr. Lewis was where do I find a job? You know, I don't have any library experience really. And he said, "The Museum of Modern Art is looking for a page. Why don't you get in touch with them?" So that was my first job. I worked at the Museum of Modern Art for eight years and later went back for another year and I went from being a page to doing cataloging and head of reference.[6]**

Connie tells another great story about the importance of books in her family:

> **Well, books were always a very important part in our family. I grew up in Berlin, Germany, during the war years. In fact the war and I started at the same time, 1939. When our family left after the war, we came to the United States, you know, to New York. My grandparents had to flee and they left everything behind and so did our family because we came over actually at the time of the airlift—the Berlin airlift—and so we brought just very basic things. And many years later, I would say fifty, over fifty years later, my husband and I opened up the crates that had been standing in my cousin's basement all those years. And out of twenty-five—twenty-five or twenty-six—huge crates, sixteen of them were filled with books. So that tells me something about the importance books had in the life of our family.**[7]

Jane Fitzpatrick, the interviewer, knows that both Connie and her husband are librarians and both went to Columbia. She assumes they met at Columbia. Connie corrects her:

> **He was in the library school at Columbia, but he was a daytime student and I was a night student so we never would have met if it hadn't been for the fact that he came to the library at the museum, and one of my colleagues there said, "Oh, there's this good-looking guy in the reading room."**[8]

Richard was "the good-looking guy in the reading room." Jane Fitzpatrick also conducts his interview. She asks him about the decision to attend library school and receives an answer very similar to Connie Corson's:

> **I decided to go to library school when I was in my final year at college and I didn't have a clue of what I wanted to do. I had been**

> **doing some research for one of the government department faculty there, doing a lot of documents research and other things in connection with a book he was writing. And when I told him—when I asked him what should I do—he said, "Well, why don't you go to library school?" And I said, "What's that?" [Laughter]**[9]

Jane asks him if he was always an avid reader: "I read a lot. Yes, I was a good reader and I enjoyed reading and I was often at the public library as a kid. I had a crush on the librarian, the public librarian of Winter Park, Florida, when I was a freshman in high school . . . Miss Charlotte Moughton."[10]

Next, Jane asks him if Miss Moughton might be available for an oral history interview. Richard reports that she has passed, but the reference room at the Winter Park Public Library is named in her honor.

Richard Corson's career was chiefly at the Luce Library at the State University of New York Maritime College, a school at Fort Schuyler in Throggs Neck, New York. This is a military college for cadets specializing in oceanography and marine engineering. Among other things, Mr. Corson was in charge of a "ship's library," a collection of materials that accompanied the cadets on voyages of their training ship.

Mrs. Corson's career took an unexpected turn. After working as a librarian at the Museum of Modern Art and then as an art bibliographer at a university, she was asked by a friend at a New York City girls' school to help with the selection committee for a new school librarian. She had never even considered school librarianship before, but after touring the school and sitting with the selection committee drawing up the job description, she decided *she* wanted the job. So her career began by following an unexpected path that led her to an even more unexpected conclusion.

Valerie Feinman was born in Canada, and her godmother was the reference librarian at the Hamilton (Ontario) Public Library. Ms. Feinman recalls that when she was eleven or twelve, her father and godmother noticed her aptitude for debate and decreed that she should be a librarian.

> This was 1950, approximately, and the day I turned fourteen, which was in 1951, I began working in the Hamilton Public Library. My godmother, Isabelle Skelly, said, "If you want to have a career in Hamilton, in Canada—anywhere—you might as well become a librarian." . . .
>
> So, I started at the public library. What does a page do? Well, I started in the summertime, so they gave me all the dirty work: unloading boxes of gift books that came in from all sorts of funny places, and arranging them alphabetically by author. . . . Many books were in sets of twenty, thirty, forty volumes on flimsy paper that were meant to grace the shelves of someone's library, but they were not meant for a public library. And one of the things I was allowed to do, besides arranging books, was to look at these sets of books, and if there was anything I like[d] there where there were two or more copies, I could have it. I have a big collection of flimsy-paper classic books dating back from that. I still have them.[11]

Later, at the Toronto library system, Ms. Feinman got to work on the bookmobiles:

> Bookmobiles [were] fun. You usually worked four days a week, from 9 to 6 on one day—two days—and 9 to 9 or 10 on the other days, because you had to go out on the buses. We had two buses, and two cabs, plus a trailer. I was mostly on that one. We were paid $3 extra every month so that we could have pants and be decorous climbing into the cab—and to pay for the dry-cleaning of said pants. [Laughing] . . .
>
> The most exciting thing was the night we were coming back across this long, eight-lane highway in a snowstorm. And the trailer decided that it wanted to go down in the ditch. And it did. And it disconnected. And the cab only went partway down. And we got out of the cab and called the police and the tow trucks, etc., and they came and pulled the cab back onto the highway so

> **that we were able to go back to the library, but the van took two or three days to dig out because it was covered with snow and deeply down.[12]**

Ultimately, Ms. Feinman became a science librarian:

> **As an undergraduate, I had studied chemistry, geology, physics, mathematics, etc. I was majoring in general sciences—this is a side story—because, again, there were no jobs for Canadian women in sciences. Once, while I was at college, my dean called me in and said, "You are not doing very well in your chemistry courses. I think that you should not want to be a chemist." And I looked him up and down, and said, "Have you been in the science library lately?" He said, "No." He was a geologist—he didn't need the library very much. I said, "Well, the books are all out of order. There's nothing published in the last three years that is a book. The journals are impossible to find. You don't have the latest journals. And there is not a science librarian. I want to become that science librarian." He said, "My blessings—continue in your courses. We'd love to have you as a science librarian."[13]**

Stories of "accidental librarians" who did not initially intend to pursue the career of librarianship are an element of the social memory occurring many times over within the corpus of interviews. Jennifer Patterson, Rita Auerbach, Peggy Richwine, Nancy Fogarty, and ALA Past President Sarah Long were all motivated to choose librarianship after initially preparing to be teachers.

Ms. Richwine, a science librarian like Ms. Feinman, chose librarianship after teaching for a few years. She very much enjoyed teaching and describes it as a rewarding experience, but for reasons she chose not to share in the interview, she found that teaching did not give her the flexibility she desired. Academic librarianship in a science department allowed her flexibility and the ability to pursue her love of the sciences.

She especially enjoyed the reference interview:

> **But—the innocence of some of the questions, and the—trying to get to the point of view of the user, of the person who is asking you the question is really, really tricky at times. And you just have to keep working with the individual until you can really say, "Oh, now I know what he's trying to find!" Sometimes it's easy and sometimes it's not. And it is really—and when you finally get it, especially when they've been beating all around the bush and not saying what it is that you think they should've been saying, you say "Oh wow."**[14]

Nancy Fogarty also chose librarianship after teaching because of the flexibility. She disliked all the grading and the rigidity of the teacher's schedule. In addition to the scheduling flexibility, librarianship appealed to her because of its many permutations: academic, school, public.

> **There were lots of papers to grade if you taught English correctly—and taught writing. And I wanted to explore other options for careers where there was more flexibility, and where you worked year round—or had the option. In librarianship I could see working in public libraries, school libraries, university, special libraries. There just seemed to be more options.**[15]

Ms. Fogarty began working as a reference intern while going to library school. After graduating she stayed on as a reference librarian, an interlibrary loan librarian, head of reference, and then library instruction coordinator.

She has always been a reader:

> **Well, I did enjoy reading. My mother returned to work when I was four years old and I began nursery school. And soon after I began, my dad picked me up one afternoon and I told him I'd been "com-**

moded" to kindergarten because I could read. Of course, I couldn't really read, I had simply memorized the books—but I really could not read at that point. . . . Everyone else thought I could, that was what was important.[16]

Rita Auerbach began her career as a high school English and history teacher. She loved the kids and loved the intellectual challenges of teaching, but she also reports disliking the rigidity of the schedule and the constant pressure to maintain a current lesson plan. She relates a story about the librarian at her school who seemed to combine the best of both worlds. This librarian had an interest in archaeology, so she arranged to teach a class just for one semester—she traded shifts with one of the teachers. For that semester she took over a high school archaeology class, and the social studies teacher staffed the library for that period.

When I was working at Garden City High School, Jean Crabtree was the high school librarian. She was the most extraordinarily bright and inspiring woman. Her last year working, she started teaching a course in archaeology because she loved archaeology. There was an arrangement made so the head of the social studies department would relieve her in the library so that she'd be free to teach. That was the kind of woman she was—to prepare all of this material for just one year. She was an inspiration and she loved being a librarian. When I was trying to think of what else I might want to do with my life, it was her encouragement that got me to go to library school.[17]

Ms. Auerbach states that librarianship "was my last choice of a job. I was sure that librarians sat around and waited for people to ask where the bathroom was, and that didn't seem like an intellectually stimulating way of life."[18] But when Ms. Auerbach was burned out with teaching, she remembered this school librarian and her example of successfully combining passions with the flexibility that librarianship afforded. "It was the best decision, short of marrying my husband, that I ever made."[19]

Jennifer Patterson had a very short career as a teacher. She ultimately found the flexibility of librarianship to be the career choice most complementary with her family planning goals:

> **Okay, I started out thinking I was going to teach and I spent one day in a seventh-grade classroom and the kids were throwing spit wads and the coach had to come in twice and I had no experience with classroom management and I really didn't understand what would be required to teach middle school English. I was just an English major and it sounded like a good idea. So I walked out of there thinking, well, I better think of something else. . . .**
>
> **[After having a child], I decided, okay what do I do now? I always liked libraries, maybe I'll see if there's a position open at Houston Public Library where I lived. And there was an evening and Saturdays job in the literature and biography department, which was perfect for me.**
>
> **So I worked that for about a year, a little bit more than a year, and by that time I had realized that it was a noncoercive way to teach, that being a reference librarian was a perfect way for me to continue to learn and to share what I knew with other people and help other people find what they were looking for without having to be a disciplinarian.**[20]

Several of the interview subjects report that their library careers were motivated by the flexibility demanded by their schedules as new mothers. Librarianship as a career was perfectly compatible with Jaye McLaughlin's and Diana Collins's family goals.

Jaye McLaughlin became a librarian after having her children. As an at-home mom, she began volunteering at her children's new elementary school where staff was setting up the library. "And I really happened to dig on this labeling books. That was exciting to me because it was the first time that I realized how they did it. And the elementary school librarian said, 'Well, why don't you go get a library degree?'"[21]

Based on this information, you might think that Ms. McLaughlin would have become a cataloger, but when her new library school advisor interviewed her and asked what kind of librarian she wanted to be, she replied, "Well, what kinds are there?" The advisor decided Ms. McLaughlin should focus on children's librarianship, and that decision proved prescient. Ms. McLaughlin has had a very fulfilling career as a children's librarian and children's department coordinator for the Fort Worth Public Library.

Among the many programs Ms. McLaughlin has supervised throughout her career, several stood out and were discussed in our interview. Her most successful programs were ones in which she learned things herself. For example, she organized a math program in which students from a local university taught mathematical concepts to her library kids in a fun way. The program was called Go Figure. While supervising the program, Ms. McLaughlin suddenly realized that she had never really understood those math concepts. "So maybe that is why I am a good children's librarian. I like to learn new things and things that are unfamiliar to me."[22]

Ms. McLaughlin also became involved with the Tejas Storytelling Association and produced an annual storytelling festival to teach educators how to finesse the art of storytelling. I asked her about the difference between a traditional storytime and storytelling:

> **Oh, try it sometime is my suggestion. When you are reading a book even to a group of children, you are constantly looking over and having to read the words, so you are holding the book so they can see it and you are turning your eyes. When you are telling a story, you are looking into their eyes, and that story becomes much more immediate to them. Many storytellers will say it is not just the storyteller but it is the audience, and you are bringing it in and you are making something magical. If the audience isn't interested, it won't happen. If the storyteller isn't any good, it won't happen. When you are reading a book, the kids are focused on the**

pictures. When you are telling a story, they might create that picture in their mind.[23]

Of course, storytelling is a lot harder than just reading a book at storytime. It takes passion and commitment. Ms. McLaughlin said that it was very difficult to learn to be a good storyteller while balancing all her other duties as a professional librarian and department head. In her retirement she has formed an association with other like-minded storytellers called Tipi Tellers.

Tipi Tellers brings a large teepee to the site to create a really special storytelling experience for young children that focuses on conservation of natural resources. The storytellers get older kids to help set up the teepee, then groups of students are invited into the tent to learn about Native American culture and to hear stories about nature and the environment. Using the tent removes the normal distractions of twenty-first-century life so the children can concentrate on the stories being told. Up to one hundred kindergartners will fit in the teepee.

Ms. McLaughlin's career began almost as an accident—she was just volunteering in her kids' elementary school—but it has been rewarding. And the tool of storytelling she learned as a children's librarian has given her a meaningful avocation in retirement.

Diana Collins is part of a long tradition in rural areas of learning the trade of librarianship by single-handedly—and very successfully—running a small library in the countryside. Though she has never possessed an MLS or attended graduate school, she shares priceless experience in her interview and demonstrates a thorough professionalism. Her education was in the trenches. And her story of librarianship also demonstrates the value and utility of professional associations and networks. When faced with issues she needed help with, she used the resources of the Texas Library Association and the Central Texas Library System.

When Ms. Collins began her career in 1979 as the librarian in Marble Falls, Texas, that institution consisted of just herself and a part-time clerk. She was volunteering at her church library when a Friends of the

Library member announced that the librarian at the public library had just had a baby and decided not to return as the director. At that time Ms. Collins's own child was turning five years old, so the timing was good to apply for the job. "And it was appealing—I mean, you get to do something you love and you get paid for it! Minimally paid for it."[24]

Ms. Collins's career as a librarian was inspired by her early love of libraries and memories of her grandmother reading to her:

> **My first—my first memory of books is my grandmother reading to us. All of us would pile into her big old bed, all the cousins, and she'd read. I don't remember the books now, I just remember the warm, cuddly feeling of being with my grandmother and my cousins, and there were probably cats and dogs on there too, and her reading. So it became very important very early.**
>
> **This was in a giant farmhouse in Missouri with four floors and there were trunks of books—steamer trunks full of books—and if I couldn't find anything else to do, I was back there in those trunks and dragging out books and reading them. And I was just always a reader and that comes from having reading as part of your life. My parents both read all of the time; no matter what else was going on, there was always a book in everybody's hand.[25]**

Ms. Collins's family moved quite a bit when she was a child, but she could always find solace in the local library:

> **I didn't know anybody and so I went to the public library because it was within walking distance. So I was down there, no telling, they probably just thought, "Oh, here she comes again," although I wouldn't have been a rowdy child. But I definitely would have made more shelving for them to do![26]**

One of Ms. Collins's favorite memories as a public library director was constructing and opening a new library building in Marble Falls, Texas. As part of the opening ceremonies, she oversaw a "book brigade" to involve the entire community in the move to the new building:

> **We saved five hundred books out of the children's section and we formed a human chain down two blocks to the new library. We passed those last five hundred books by hand down. And we had everybody in town and we had a cake and the rain held off until after it was over. . . . There are still people who are talking about being in the book brigade. We had Brownies, we had Cubs, we had cheerleaders, we had football team people, we had every fraternity, sorority, every public service group in town. We had teachers and firemen and city officials and we had a few county officials. And it was organized by a couple of volunteers, and actually that volunteer is our county judge . . . and she says of all the things she's ever done, that book brigade was the best. You know, so it was a very triumphant moment to go symbolically as well as physically from the old to the new. It was great fun.[27]**

Jeannette Larson had also volunteered at a school library. She was at loose ends after completing her undergraduate degree and knew she would need an additional degree to find work, but she did not want to pursue an advanced degree in anthropology. Her mother was working in a school library, and Ms. Larson accompanied her as a volunteer.

> **My undergraduate degree was from the University of New Mexico and it was in anthropology, specifically Native American studies. Which I told people later, that means I know a little bit about everything and not much about anything because it was really broad. And so I sort of finished up school and thought okay now what do I want to do? I knew I didn't want to go on and get a master's or doctorate in anthropology, and so I started thinking about what I was going to do. And [I] had a chance to volunteer at a school where my mother was working in the library and it was**

> **sort of one of those V8 moments where you kind of bonk yourself on the head and I said, "I love reading and I love being in libraries and I love doing research, why haven't I thought about working in a library?"[28]**

Library work was a good fit for Ms. Larson because it afforded flexibility. She recalls a time when she was burned out doing storytimes. But because there are so many facets of librarianship—and a modern library requires so many different types of duties—she was able to move into a management position to help train the storytime librarians.

> **Well, I think that I've been fortunate in working in libraries where I have a lot of flexibility. But also I've pushed for new projects, different projects, trying things that kind of kept the passion alive. And I think that in part because I made the efforts to go out and do things and I was willing to say, "Yeah, let me jump in and work with that," even though it was sort of outside of the perimeters of what I thought librarianship was supposed to be, it brought some really great opportunities to work with some fabulous people and to do some really fun projects that just kind of let you keep that passion alive and not just get into that "I only want to do what I was paid to do." Which, you know, I do hear from some people. . . . And I think a lot of people do come into any profession [saying,] "Okay, I'm doing what I'm paid to do." And no, you have to sometimes say, "Sure, I'll help with that," even though it's not in my job description. I think the rewards for doing that are great.[29]**

Ms. Larson's interview has many great stories about library service—and not to just the traditional library patrons, but also the "difficult" ones. She relates a story of her time at the Anaheim, California, public library when the staff was afraid of the Hell's Angel biker who had walked in the door. But—with a little trepidation—she met him at the reference desk to see what he needed. And his information and referral requests were just like everyone else's. He turned out to be a very polite and respectful patron:

> **The guy ended up being a really nice guy and was very happy that somebody was willing to help him and didn't act scared and scornful of him. And I think the same thing happens a lot of the time with homeless people. I think it is a part of public service that there are times that we have to work with stinky people. You know, get over it, there are worse things in the world. . . .**
>
> **When I talk to librarians about summer reading club, it's not the little Jeannettes of the world that needed summer reading club—I was going to read no matter what. It's the kid that doesn't know that they're going to like reading, it's the kid who doesn't think that they've ever had the right to come in and take out a book that need our services. And I think that's what we've been doing and I think we'll continue to do it even more so.[30]**

Ms. Larson is a great public library advocate. Her retirement consists of library consulting work and writing books on best library practices.

Other librarians report similar happenstance stories of their introduction to the vocation. Janet Swan Hill became a librarian because her husband was drafted during the Vietnam War and she went to live with her parents. Two of her college roommates had gone on to library school—and she was at loose ends. Library school was simply convenient. But the career was very rewarding. She was able to use her natural sciences background to become a noted geography and cartography cataloger at the Library of Congress and serve on many ALA committees and ALA Council.

John Mitchell is another accidental librarian. He was working for an engineering company, using his knowledge of Slavic languages, when the company lost its contract with the Navy. He had a friend at the Library of Congress who knew the library was desperate for a bibliographer with that language skill set. The library hired him and then he went to library school for his MLS.

Dr. Kenneth Yamashita did not intend to work in libraries. He went to the local public library looking for a temporary job as a clerk. His undergraduate work was in English literature at Indiana University, and he was working on a graduate degree in art history, but he realized that museum jobs were difficult to find, so he made an appointment with the director of the Montclair Public Library in New Jersey, Arthur Curley, to discuss library work. Mr. Curley (a past president of the American Library Association) was enthusiastic about young Mr. Yamashita's prospects and encouraged him to apply at Rutgers for a library degree:

> **It was 1971, and he was instrumental in getting me into Rutgers. He—in this interview, he got on the phone with the dean of the library school and said, "I have this wonderful candidate here who has master's credits in research and could those be applied to a master's degree in library science?" Up until that point, you know, librarianship was not a career that I had thought about, but he talked about "Well, this is a way that you could give back to your community," and I was—I was kind of perplexed because in Montclair, New Jersey, there really wasn't a community—an Asian American community—to give back to. But I think he was speaking broadly about communities of color. There was a large African American population in Montclair. So then he gave me a part-time job, a work-study job. And then when I started library school—I commuted to New Brunswick for my classes—he gave me a full-time job as a librarian intern.**[31]

Dr. Yamashita has fulfilled Mr. Curley's vision for him "giving back to the community." He worked with Loriene Roy on the ALA Spectrum Program, which provides mentoring and scholarships to minority students pursuing library degrees. Dr. Yamashita has also worked on committees for the Office for Literacy and Outreach Services as well as an initiative to diversify the staff of ALA. In professional positions at the Montclair and Chicago public libraries—and then later in California—he worked to create readers and library users within communities that were not traditionally patrons or scholars.

He holds a unique position within librarianship, having witnessed the inclusion of diverse cultures within libraries—and among the publishers of the books that we may now add to our collections. When I asked him about the difference—especially in children's literature—between the library of his childhood and the library of today, he not only noted one particular author of whom he is very proud because of a personal connection but also gave a surprising account of the other part of the sociological equation.

Dr. Yamashita was born in Utah during World War II in a Japanese American concentration camp (Topaz Relocation Center). But he grew up in Bergenfield, New Jersey, and really had no memories of his very early childhood in Utah. And his parents never discussed it.

> **When I was growing up, the camp experience was not mentioned in my family. When my mother or father would say, "Well, when we were in camp blah, blah, blah," we thought they were talking about summer camp and not concentration camp, so it was not a topic that was discussed.**[32]

He talks about the work of Yoshiko Uchida, who accurately depicted the concentration camp in a series of young adult novels, *Journey to Topaz* and *Journey Home,* and an autobiography, *Desert Exile.* He is grateful for these books that were published in the 1970s but also knows the audience for these materials may not have been ready for them until that time. Here he describes the library of his childhood:

> **I think that the big difference would be in a child like myself, a person of color. I think they would be surprised that there were**

> **no children's books or stories that were about their particular ethnic group. And certainly if their parents wanted them to read stories about their particular ethnic group or language group, they wouldn't find those materials. . . . But it is interesting because of the experience of Japanese Americans during the war, most Japanese Americans wanted—especially the parents wanted—the children to become fully Americanized. So we weren't looking for materials about our ethnic group. We wanted to read about, you know, the majority community's experiences.[33]**

Dr. Yamashita's retirement from the Stockton library came during a painful recession in California. He describes San Joaquin County as the epicenter of the subprime mortgage crisis, and his library system was dependent on property taxes that could no longer be collected because of all the foreclosures. In talking about the difficult decisions that were made during his last years as director, he stresses an important aspect of librarianship: the library's human resources. It is easy to think of the library as a collection of materials and that access to the materials—the hours of operation—is the most essential component of a library. But during his management of the financial crisis, Dr. Yamashita strove to preserve the staff. "The staff is really the most valuable commodity."[34] Everything else could be replaced after the crisis was over.

Kathy Kaya also started her career as a clerk. She says, "I entered the profession sort of through the back door." She was drawn to the field of librarianship because when she was working as a Spanish teacher part-time at the university in Bozeman, Montana, she simply really liked interacting with the librarians at the main library. "I wanted to be like them." She stayed with library work because of the relationships she could cultivate.

Ms. Kaya's husband was a professor, and when he took a sabbatical in Hawaii to do some research, she took the opportunity to attend library school in Honolulu. And she enjoyed her life as a librarian much more than that of a part-time Spanish teacher.

Academic librarianship was the right career for Kathy Kaya because she was able to cultivate two types of professional relationships: those with the professors, maintaining and developing a corpus of material to support their scholarly needs, and those with the students, who needed bibliographic instruction and support to complete their research.

> **I made it a point to establish relationships with the faculty. So if I saw books in our review area that might be of interest, I would send them a note or an e-mail, or call them. And I would contact individual [professors] to find out what their projects were—if there were ways we could work together. They would send their classes in—or individual students in—with questions and to work with me.**
>
> **And, even at the reference desk instead of, you know, there was a lot of just providing answers and instruction, but I was able to develop relationships with, for example, graduate students so they kept coming back and coming back. And so there is a contractor in town who still thanks me every day after thirty years. Every time he sees me, he thanks me for helping him get his master's degree. Because he was my student.**[35]

Sheila Ross Henderson worked as a clerk in the medical library at M. D. Anderson Hospital in Houston, Texas, the summer before she planned to enter nursing school. "It was quite by accident." She found the library so fascinating that she never made it to nursing school. She stayed at the medical library for eight years before going to library school for her MLIS. Hers was the first class to graduate with the "Information Science" designation. After working in the medical library, she went on to lead public libraries in Georgetown and Brenham, Texas, and then an academic library.

In each of her libraries, Ms. Henderson has endeavored to instill a culture of service. Her interview was punctuated not just with personal stories about leading a library with good customer service but also with examples of her own tactics to address the underserved patrons at her libraries.

> **I think the most important thing I learned at library school was that if you are not service-oriented, you are probably in the wrong profession. And I took that to heart and I have applied that everywhere I have been. . . .**
>
> **The customer is always going to be a human being. [Laughter] And so those—those skills, those negotiating skills, are very important. You know, it doesn't matter whether I am right, the customer is always right until I can convince the customer that my way is the better way. And if that does not happen, it is still up to me to make sure that there is, you know, a fair exchange and that the customer feels like I have been fair with him.**[36]

Ms. Henderson shares a story of a troublesome child from when she worked in Brenham. The young man would show up after school with his gang of rabble-rousers to terrorize the library. He "lived to come to the library and create problems for the staff. That was the highlight of his day."[37] Finally he was pulled into the director's office where Ms. Henderson found that he did not have a library card—and was living with an elderly guardian who was not likely to come in and sign for his card. So Ms. Henderson said, "Okay, here is what I am going to do for you. I am going to give you a book and I want you to read it and when you finish reading the book, I want you to return it to me and we will talk about it."[38] She gave the boy the positive attention he craved and eventually trusted him with a library card. She turned that boy into a reader who valued the library. He stayed, but his gang disappeared.

At the Georgetown (Texas) Public Library she faced a similar situation with a young girl:

> **Her language, oh my gosh. Yeah. [Laughter] And she was—she too was one that lived for frustrating the staff. At my first staff meet-**

> **ing I was told about this young lady. She would come in the library with her friends and she would get so rowdy that they would have to throw her out. It was a ritual. Well, I decided we weren't going to have that ritual. So I asked about her parents. Well, it turns out that her grandmother—she is living with her grandmother and the grandmother was quite a colorful character herself. [Laughter] So I had to go start with the grandmother. I went to meet the grandmother and because I was their first African American library director, they were very pleased to have me in the community so she was very respectful of me.[39]**

Ms. Henderson met with the girl and her grandmother and offered a deal: if the young girl behaved in the library—and if her grades improved at school—at the end of the school year Ms. Henderson would take her to Merle Norman's for a makeover. And that girl became a model library user, encouraging better behavior from her friends as well.

Ms. Henderson was not afraid of leaving the confines of the building to lead her library. She relates a story about how she identified several for-profit businesses in her community that were providing excellent customer service. She arranged field days for her management staff to go out and meet these business leaders to discuss how they kept their customers happy and devoted.

She was also adept at pulling in community leaders who were initially skeptical of her leadership and the library's mission. She talks about identifying reluctant library board members and Friends of the Library members and putting them in positions of leadership so that they worked with her to benefit the whole library. Much of her interview discusses staff development in the same manner. When faced with a truculent adversary—whether that person is a patron, community leader, or staff member—she works to make him or her a partner in the library's mission.

Robert Gaines began his librarian career as a doctoral student in history and along the way worked as a student assistant at the Vanderbilt library. Like many PhD candidates, he taught undergraduate classes while contemplating his dissertation, and it was during this time that he realized his abysmal job prospects as a history professor. So he abandoned his dissertation and instead went to library school at the University of Tennessee at Knoxville in 1973. He was hired at the University of North Carolina at Greensboro immediately after graduation and has had a successful career there:

> **When it looked as though the employment opportunities were going to be few and far between, library science for me was a natural fallback—and a very congenial fallback because I've enjoyed working at libraries and you still get to teach, quite a bit.**[40]

Mr. Gaines reflects on how good reference work is not unlike teaching—and has the same rewards—but on an individual level:

> **Teaching and bibliographic instruction has always been close to my heart and it takes me back to the actual classroom teaching which I began my career doing, teaching history in higher education. But at the same time, I honestly believe that the one-on-one communication with an individual patron in which you successfully solve a problem for that patron—and provide that patron with good information and they leave happy and well-prepared to answer their question or write their paper—that's fulfilling, in and of itself. . . . That's always very fulfilling and it can happen tens of thousands of times in a library career.**[41]

Librarianship was a fulfilling career for Mr. Gaines because of the interactions with students and faculty, but also because it forced him to keep acquiring new knowledge and reference skills: he was able to be both teacher and student. In another passage referring to his mentor, Nancy Fogarty, he discusses the art of reference work:

> **There are circumstances in which a question would be asked and she's worked with the materials so long that she can come up with a very esoteric source that's on a shelf fifty feet away that I just wasn't familiar with. And that really comes from long service. It can't be done from coursework. I think that really comes from long service and really applying yourself to learning your collection. And learning your collection is part of really becoming an effective librarian. Know what you have. And if you don't have the best sources, buy the best sources—find out what's out there, the new materials that are out there that can help you do your job better.[42]**

Sandy Berman is a well-known social activist and cataloging maven, but the genesis of his library career was quite inauspicious. He grew up in Los Angeles and spent a great deal of time at the La Cienega branch of the public library. He spent so much time there that he decided that he wanted a job; however, the librarian at the time did not like hiring boys as pages. But he persisted:

> **I just, you know, I just kept on showing up, saying I really wanted to work here and whatever, and so she ultimately relented and I count that as a kind of breaking a sex barrier of sorts. . . . So that's how I got into libraries the first time and I want to say that my first job, absolutely first job—messenger clerk, seventy-five cents an hour at La Cienega Branch Public Library—somebody handed me a mop, pointed to the fairy tale section in the children's area and said "Clean it up" because a little kid had peed on the floor.**
>
> **So that was the commencement of my professional career, and I figure you can only rise from that point. It can only get better, right?[43]**

After a stint in the Army, Mr. Berman found himself visiting the public library in Washington, D.C., and noticed a sign posted on a bulletin board about a work-study program in conjunction with Catholic University. He enrolled in the MSLS program and began working at the District of Columbia Public Library in the acquisitions department. His life as a professional librarian took off from there, landing at various points back in California at UCLA and finally at the Hennepin County (Minnesota) Library system. But there were also two years spent in Zambia and two years spent in Uganda.

Mr. Berman is primarily known for his contributions to subject authority work. Among progressive catalogers, he is well regarded for his sharp criticism of Library of Congress subject authority records that have a Western bias or are insensitive to matters of race, ethnicity, and sexuality. His time spent in Africa crystallized this mission for Mr. Berman. He even calls it a "cataloging fixation, if not crusade":

> **For instance, the term *kafirs* was used routinely way back then. This was 1969, '70, '71 I am speaking of. It was used routinely to refer to black people in South Africa, where really what they meant was Zulu, or any number of ethnic groups. And on investigation—and in fact this investigation didn't have to go further than one or two other people—you realize that this was insulting language and derived from the Arabic meaning "infidel." There was nothing good about it. There was nothing even neutral. It was totally negative. It was that kind of discovery—revelation—that moved me, actually appalled me.**[44]

Mr. Berman's career as a librarian has been about providing access to knowledge. He sums it up eloquently:

> **Coming to work every day we are actually in the business—and had the opportunity and the pleasure—of liberating materials by making them more accessible, more comprehensible to the people who are using the library and to our colleagues, particularly on the reference desk and readers' advisory.**[45]

Micki Freeny's library career also began in high school when she worked as a page at the public library.

> **[It was] one of those things where I was going to either work at the A&W Root Beer place or the library—and I got the job at the library. And they were nice enough to give me a job every summer all through college. I was able to come back and work at Christmas, as well.[46]**

Like many librarians, Ms. Freeny initially thought she would be a schoolteacher and studied French as an undergraduate. After graduation she moved to France and taught at two French schools.

> **And while I was there, I learned enough that I didn't want to be a teacher. . . . I found that almost all I did was discipline. And I thought, I don't want to go back and teach French. My experience in high school was that most people didn't like French. So here's something that I loved, so did I want to go back to an American high school and try to teach something that I loved to people who hated it and know that 80 or 90 percent of what I did would just be pure discipline and not teaching?**
>
> **And so I thought, I've got to do something else. . . . I had worked in the library and I thought, "Well, I really like the public library."**
>
> **I knew of two library schools. Back then, we didn't have the Internet, I didn't know how to—it wasn't easy to research. I knew of Catholic University and the University of Maryland. When the University of Maryland application came, you had to do it in triplicate. And it was like, "Well, I really don't want to go that bad." So I threw it away.**
>
> **Catholic University's came, and it had nice, soft—"What was the last book you read you liked?" It was fun to fill out. So I completed it, sent it in, and lo and behold I got accepted without having done things like sending in my GREs, or—and my mother said she would loan me the money to go, so . . . .**

So I went, and finished in two summers and a year—finished in one year plus a summer. . . . Prince George's County gave me an interview, I got the job.

And I can remember how excited I was. I took a Metro bus back to my apartment in the District, and I can remember talking to the bus driver about how I had gotten this job—I was the only person on the bus—and he said, "Well, how much are you going to make?" And I said, "Nine thousand dollars."

"Nine thousand dollars!?" He said, "I make more than that! You have a master's degree and you're going to work for nine thousand dollars?"

That kind of burst my balloon, but I loved it from the very beginning.[47]

Andrew Hansen's career had begun in public libraries after working for a school library while in high school. Later, when he was working to pay tuition for college, he applied at the Omaha (Nebraska) Public Library:

I was told that they were looking for a shelver in the children's department of the Omaha main public library. I applied on a hot, late August day for the job, wearing a shirt—a white shirt—and a necktie. And fifteen minutes later, I was taking care of a backlog of children's books . . . that hadn't been shelved—because they were lacking a page—for a while.[48]

Mr. Hansen worked at the Omaha library for all four years of his college education, but never considered becoming a librarian. After college Mr. Hansen went into the Air Force for four years but planned to be a math teacher after finishing his tour. He had completed all the necessary courses, and he just needed to apply for a teaching certificate.

And one Sunday afternoon I laid down [to] take a nap in the barracks. When I woke up, the decision had been made: I was gonna use the GI Bill and get a library degree—become a librarian. The

encouragement that I had received while I had been working in the Omaha Public Library had just fallen on deaf ears for most of the—well, all of the time that I was working there. And I suddenly woke up and realized that this was the direction I wanted to go. So I applied and was accepted at the University of Minnesota library school. I enrolled there. This was in the summer of 1955.[49]

Mr. Hansen worked at the Bismarck (North Dakota) and Sioux City (Iowa) public libraries before taking an administrative position with the American Library Association, so he has perspectives on librarianship from both the front lines of public service and a national advocacy organization. He discussed several changes in the profession during his tenure, but two stood out and are interrelated. The first concerns the nature and the process of interlibrary loan.

When Mr. Hansen began his career, an interlibrary loan request had to be for "legitimate" research purposes, and the process was opaque. The librarian would grill the requester about his intentions, perhaps because of all the work that would have to be done to secure the loan: first filling in the "three-part ALA form" and then sending it blindly to an institution that might own the book—and might deem it available for loan. The revolution in interlibrary loan practices—and the technology that made the process transparent—is especially appreciated by Mr. Hansen.

The other issue that Mr. Hansen addressed was censorship. He tells several stories about intellectual freedom. The first one is from his earliest days as a public library director. A local conservative group donated a book that he did not want to accession. Back then the ALA's Library Bill of Rights included the following language to describe what should be protected: "books of sound factual authority." The book in question was a political tract of very dubious merit, full of factual errors. But the question was raised to the library board, and the board asked that the book be added—over the young librarian's objections.

As he progressed in his career, Mr. Hansen saw the error in his original view, and he notes that the ALA also amended the Library Bill of Rights to remove that phrase, because it invited the very sort of censorship that is anathema to a free society.

The interlibrary loan memories and the censorship discussions are interrelated because they both show a progression in library philosophy from restrictive (and judgmental) librarianship to the modern library as a place for all knowledge to be shared.

Mr. Hansen also has a Mark Twain–esque view of the arc of his career. Upon arriving as the director of the Bismarck Public Library in 1957, he was told by his predecessor that a decision to purchase the controversial novel *Peyton Place* had not been made because any fallout about the acquisition would land in the new director's lap. Mr. Hansen ordered the book—and found that the only real complaint was that the reserve queue for it was so long (and he refused to buy extra copies until they came out in paperback).

And then at the end of his career, he saw an article in a library professional journal about weeding items that have some cultural import but are simply no longer circulating. The article was titled "Is It Time to Weed *Peyton Place*?"

> **And it kinda hit me—because I remembered a movie when I was a child—that Mark Twain was born under Halley's Comet, and he died under Halley's Comet. I thought, ya know, my first job at a library was to buy *Peyton Place,* and if it is time to weed it, this is my Halley's comet.**[50]

Not all librarians are "accidental" librarians, though. Many of the interviewees knew from their earliest years that they desired this profession. Gail Hueting reports she knew in the eighth grade that she wanted to work in a library. She did not think this was possible because of her profound hearing disability—and she was under the impression that all librarians were reference librarians, working with patrons. In high school, though, the school librarian introduced her to cataloging and the technical services side of librarianship, which proved to be a very fulfilling career for Ms. Hueting.

> **Well, I've always been a cataloger, even though the titles may not say that. And this goes back to when I was in high school, and I was a library assistant. I became interested in library work as a career in eighth grade, junior high, anyway, but the problem was that my hearing was impaired, so I wasn't sure whether I could be a reference librarian, and the high school librarian, for whom I was a student worker, said she thought I might like to go into cataloging.**[51]

And cataloging has been the perfect career for Gail Hueting. Her interview shows how librarianship—and cataloging in particular—enabled her to use her research and mastery of languages even though she is deaf. And not all of her time has been spent in the back rooms of technical services. She is adept at lipreading and has always taken shifts at the reference desk. "I don't consider myself a very good reference librarian. Sometimes I can find information that a person needs, but unfortunately sometimes I think of the place to find the answer when they've given up and gone out the door!"[52]

Ms. Hueting can truly appreciate the gifts of technology in library science. Her career was almost cut short during her first internship in library school when she spent an entire summer interfiling catalog cards to address a multiyear filing backlog. She finds it humorous when people complain about the patron interface of the OPAC, because she can very well remember when there was but one catalog, and it was never up to date.

Ms. Hueting brought several items from her cataloger's desk for the interview. Her institution used primarily Library of Congress classification for the bulk of the collection, but some of the modern language collections used Dewey Decimal Classification (DDC)—and an in-house hybrid of the two systems based on the DDC Shakespeare tables. At the time of this interview, libraries were using DDC23, but Ms. Hueting wanted to make a point about the importance of documenting cataloging practices—especially when they are bespoke and adapted for a particular collection. She brought her copy of the sixteenth edition of Dewey, because it is the one she inherited from the previous cataloger. It holds the "margin notes" and annotations to unlock the secrets of the University of Illinois's classification procedures for foreign literature. She also brought a vintage Cutter Three-Figure Author Table.

Gail Hueting has enjoyed her career as a cataloger. It was a perfect fit for her interest in languages and her hearing impairment. She does note—a bit wistfully—that she wishes the electronic age had ushered e-mail and chat into our profession sooner, because they made communication so much easier for her.

Dr. Arlene Luster knew she wanted to be a librarian at an even earlier age. She has a strong memory from when she was four years old and her mother took her to the library:

> **And I couldn't even see over the top of the counter. It was really high. And I saw this lady, and she probably wasn't a librarian, maybe she was a circulation clerk—I'm not sure. She had this pencil and a stamp pad. And she took the pencil, and it was attached to the pencil, ok, the little stamp pad. And she stamped it, she turned the pencil around.**
>
> **And as soon as I saw that, I was convinced. I wanted to be a librarian. And when I went to high school, the school had a field trip down to the public library. And we went to the teen section, and this young adult librarian read the book *Momma's Bank Account.* I was doubly convinced that I wanted to be a librarian. And that's why. That's why really. That's why.**[53]

Later in the interview, when Dr. Luster is talking about technological change in the profession, she laughs and reports that she never got to use that little rubber stamp. She never got to use it even though it was the inspiration for her whole career.

Dr. Irene Hoadley also knew she would be a librarian from an early age:

> **I guess I was one of those people of my generation that intuitively knew at a very early age that I wanted to be a librarian. Not because I'd really had any experiences in libraries—because I grew up in a very small community—there was no public library. The library in the school, the elementary school I went to was one little-bitty bookcase, and in the high school it wasn't a great deal more than that. But I always liked to read, and I had an appreciation of books, and so I thought—there wasn't anything else I really wanted to do. . . . And there was no question, having grown up in a small town, that I didn't want to stay there. I wanted a career. I wanted to be able to do something else with my life. And so, this seemed like a good fit for me.**[54]

Though she ultimately received a PhD from the library school at the University of Michigan, Dr. Hoadley never really considered teaching. She has always felt comfortable managing, and she was an administrator for several academic libraries before taking the directorship at Texas A&M.

> **I always probably considered myself a manager. My mother said I could manage a broomstick. I guess I always felt very comfortable being in charge. And when you feel that way, then I think that's something that you naturally progress to. And it was also probably at a time in the profession where there were not many women in library administration—and I always hate a void—and it was just a natural progression.**[55]

She did not "break the glass ceiling" as the first woman director of an ARL (Association of Research Libraries) institution—she believes there were three or four women in the United States before her—but her effectiveness as a leader must be pronounced because she became the director at A&M, a school with a long history of educating military cadets and which had only recently become coeducational when Dr. Hoadley joined the staff in 1974.

Dr. Hoadley's career is uniquely positioned in the world of technology. In her early years working in Ohio, she was directed to help craft a proposal to share resources with an electronic union catalog. She worked with a small team to envision an interlibrary loan network. And that seminal draft proposal—which she was tasked with writing—eventually became OCLC.

She was also instrumental in automating the Texas A&M library and creating technology labs on campus for student use. However, she was of an era that considered the actual, everyday use of a computer better left to administrative assistants and clerical staff. Even when she retired in 1992, Dr. Hoadley still did not have a computer in her office.

The *Capturing Our Stories* project debuted at the beginning of Loriene Roy's ALA presidency in 2008 with a preconference workshop on oral history methodology in Anaheim. Sarah Long and Ninfa Trejo interviewed each other immediately after the workshop that day. And they both went on to be some of the best advocates for the project at the conference.

Sarah Long began her career as a teacher, but she readily admits to having failed in that role. In librarianship she found her gift for working with children—and she was very successful as a children's librarian. She led many large public libraries and has served as president of the Public Library Association and the American Library Association. However, as her administrative responsibilities grew, she was not quite sure she was ready to work with adults as the director of a library:

> **It made me very nervous at first, because I was used to working with children. And while I've always been able to talk easily, I got so nervous that I would write out these little cards for opening ceremonies. "Hello, my name is Sarah Long. I am the director of the library." I was very nervous about coming across as adult and**

in charge and not being a children's person. All of my friends had warned me that I would have to give up my feather boas and my cowboy boots and other crazy costumes that I had adopted as a children's librarian. And I did for a while, but now I'm back to dressing up again. Anyway, I got along pretty well being a public library director. . . .

I think actually working with youth is pretty good preparation for being an administrator. If you can organize a program for kids, you can certainly organize a board meeting. Now I'm not meaning to put down board members, but it's a similar kind of thing. If you can organize volunteers to work with the children's program, you can recruit people to help you in any kind of management exercise you'd like to mention. So I think that if you can work with young people, you can just about work with anybody. And children's librarians are legendary for being able to find the resources and convince people to help them for harebrained projects.

And a lot of what you do as an administrator, at some level, can be considered a harebrained project. So I think that in many ways I was well suited to move up into library administration.[56]

Ms. Long has had a successful career as a librarian, as an administrator, and as the public face of large organizations because she is able to empathize. When discussing her management strategy, she advocates kindness:

Librarians are employers, and when you get into an employment situation there're many—you can get into many difficult situations. One has to have policies and to be careful, and so on and so forth. I would put a strong oar in for kindness and for listening to others, and for trying to see things from other people's point of view.

And I think a lot can be helped by this approach and by trying to put yourself in another person's shoes, even if you have bad news to deliver. Whatever you can do to ease the path. So many times when you look back in history, you can see where countries got

into trouble because somebody's pride was hurt. And if you can protect people's pride, if you can give people a graceful way out, oftentimes that goes a long way.[57]

Sarah Long and Ninfa Trejo interviewed each other, and they have been colleagues for many years. This relationship shines through in the course of their interviews. In fact, Ms. Long opens Ms. Trejo's interview by saying, "It's so nice to see you. I always enjoy seeing old friends at these conferences. Isn't that one of the reasons we come?"[58]

Ms. Trejo came to librarianship in middle age, after careers in public policy (working for Jerry Brown the first time he was governor of California), bilingual education, and public relations. While working at the San Diego (California) Public Library as public relations officer, she decided to pursue a library degree: "I fell in love with the work librarians do. And I thought, 'This is what I want to do.'"[59]

San Diego did not have a library school at that time, but Ms. Trejo found that San José State University was offering a master's degree program at the Fullerton extension campus. The deal was sealed when she came to work one day at the San Diego Public Library and found that someone had left a flyer on her desk describing a position in Fullerton: "They needed a Hispanic liaison at the Fullerton Public Library—and they described just who I was." She went to work in Fullerton and began library school to launch her third career.

Much of the interview revolves around Ms. Trejo's romance with and marriage to an esteemed librarian, library professor, and scholar of Hispanic culture, Dr. Arnulfo Duenes Trejo. Ms. Long also knew Dr. Trejo, who died in 2003, and counted him a friend, so the two women shared memories of him and his contributions to librarianship. Ninfa Trejo met her future husband at a library conference in Anaheim, California, where they were both attending a supper for REFORMA (The National Association to Promote Library and Information Services to Latinos and the Spanish-Speaking). They exchanged brief introductions at the supper and then saw each other twice at the conference. At the close of the conference, Arnulfo asked Ninfa if she would have supper with him, but she told him she needed to get back to San Diego because she had committed to taking her teenage son to Mass that evening. Dr. Trejo inquired which church she attended—and then sat behind her that night at Mass.

She and Dr. Trejo shared a late-in-life love affair that revolved around libraries and Hispanic culture. Ms. Trejo continues Arnulfo's work with the Trejo Foster Foundation by hosting institutes to promote the education of librarians and bridge cultural understanding.

Pat Tuohy began thinking about becoming a librarian as she was finishing up her undergraduate work in Latin American Studies at the University of Texas (UT) in 1970. At that time the library school was housed with the library on the third floor of the Main Building (the UT Tower). The section of the library that composed the Latin American collection was also on the third floor of the Tower.

> **And we shared a corridor and a bathroom with the library school when it was there on the third floor, and I hung out in the hallway with the Cokes, because you couldn't take those into the library. I talked with library students and asked them, "What's library school all about?" And I can't even tell you who these people were, but they were enthusiastic about library school. And what was most appealing to me is how you get to stay in libraries and hang out in libraries—and since my life was revolving around the Latin American collection, I thought, oh wee, that would be wonderful to just hang out here and get paid for it.**[60]

In library school Ms. Tuohy was mentored by Dr. Billie Grace Herring, and she also speaks fondly of Sam Witten, another beloved Texas library educator:

> **He was a legend among the old-timers in the library school. He taught public libraries, he taught publishing, he taught library history, and he was a non-PhD. He was a practicing public librar-**

> **ian who had spent many years on the reference desk and head of reference at Dallas Public. He knew public libraries, he knew reference, he knew people, he knew the organization, he knew the rough and tumble of public libraries which are very out-front-in-your-face political—and they always have been. We pretend as public librarians that we're above the fray but we're not, we're right down there with police, fire, scraping for money. We're in the public arena, and Sam was very forthright about the need for public librarians, or all librarians really, to get involved and to try to influence the political process for the favor or to the benefit of public libraries. . . .**
>
> **His most powerful message—that I can clearly remember—was the obligation—the sacred duty, no less—sacred duty to preserve and promote and guard intellectual freedom in the public library setting. Intellectual freedom is a core principle of public librarianship, and we as librarians have to defend it even though we may not agree—or are scared to death about what it's going to do to our career or our job or that we could lose whatever job we're in trying to defend intellectual freedom. It was a sacred duty founded on those core American values and principles. And he taught that the most basic element of public librarianship was preservation of intellectual freedom—and going to the mat for it.**[61]

The interviewer then asks whether Ms. Tuohy had ever had to "go to the mat" to defend intellectual freedom, and she relates a story about her early days at CTLS (Central Texas Library System, now Connecting Texas Libraries Statewide), when she was responsible for acquiring the 16 mm films that the system loaned to the member libraries for their children's programming. The individual regional systems—though they were state funded—were administered by the large public library in each region. The Austin Public Library originally administered CTLS. Austin and its city government have always been very progressive, so in the 1980s the City of Austin adopted an ordinance prohibiting the municipal government from doing business with any vendor that also traded with South Africa. This measure was meant to pressure the government of South Africa to renounce apartheid. As it happened, two of the library's vendors were also trading with South Africa: the publishers of the *Encyclopaedia Britannica* and the distributors of Disney films, Buena Vista.

After agonizing with a colleague about how to defend intellectual freedom while balancing the horrors of apartheid, Ms. Tuohy and her associate decided to take their case to the city council. Ms. Tuohy recalls that it was a scary time to stand up to the city manager and council, and both librarians knew it might jeopardize their career development opportunities. But they did it: they got an exemption from the ordinance because it was a clear case of censorship. And the children of central Texas were not deprived of the latest Disney films!

Pat Tuohy has been a leader and sage counsel for countless librarians in Texas throughout her career because she models the ideals of librarianship that she learned from her mentors and because she understands how state and local governments work.

Here, Pat Tuohy shares a library school memory involving Dr. Herring, another beloved professor at the Texas library school. Ms. Tuohy has just been asked why she did not pursue academic librarianship, and she responds:

> **Cataloging. Let's be perfectly clear, it was cataloging. It was AACR1, it wasn't even 2 [AACR2] . . . but it was a prerequisite for academic libraries, and I knew I couldn't make the cut because I could barely make a B in Billie Grace Herring's beginning cataloging course. And Billie Grace Herring needs to be interviewed for this because she is a wonderful library school teacher. You need to interview her very soon—she is a wonderful woman. She guided the careers and positively influenced library school students for years and years.**
>
> **And I owe her an incredible debt because I didn't earn a B in that class, but she saw in me a love of libraries and she really gave**

> **me a B, which is exactly what you had to have. And I'm eternally grateful to her. She wouldn't remember this, but I of course do.[62]**

The interviewer then asks, "What was it about her that made her so wonderful and inspiring?"

> **Well, a very genuine, caring person. I believe she was a lecturer at that time working on a PhD in library science at the university. But she really cared about students. . . . And when I told her I was much more interested in public libraries—she was very enthusiastic about that change and she said, "Yes, you would be a great public librarian and I think that's a good career choice for you to pursue." A wonderful advisor, a wonderful teacher, and a great library humanitarian.[63]**

Dr. Billie Grace Herring is a library school professor beloved by several generations of librarians who attended UT at Austin. I was prompted by many people to seek her out as a subject for this oral history project.

Billie Grace Herring began her library career by accident—while chatting with the school superintendent in line at the grocery store. Dr. Herring had prepared for a career as a teacher and then married and had children and expected to be a full-time homemaker. But this lifestyle did not agree with her:

> **Our second son had been born and I was just not happy being a hausfrau. I needed something more stimulating, so I worked for an abstract company for a while typing oil leases—which was absolutely deadly. I knew I was going to have to get back to school and do something, but I didn't particularly want to teach in a classroom at that point. So I was in the grocery store one day, the only big grocery store in town, and I was in the checkout line behind the superintendent of schools. I told him that I wanted to come in and talk with him about substitute teaching for them the next year.**

> **He said, "Substitute teaching?! I need a librarian for the junior high school. Do you have any hours in library science?" Well, I had three, but it turned out I was able to return to Austin and take courses that summer.**[64]

So Dr. Herring became a school librarian, almost by happenstance. She got the certification the school required that first summer and then returned to library school the next summer to take more courses. When her husband also needed to return to Austin to pursue a divinity degree at the seminary, she moved her entire family to Austin and secured another position as school librarian while continuing to finish her master's at the library school.

When she finished her master's thesis, her advisor informed her that the dean would like her to come in for a meeting. It was 1967, and the library school had been awarded several federal grants for doctoral students—and was desperate for faculty to teach. The dean recruited her to take advantage of a federal Title IIB grant at the library school and continue her research on school libraries for a doctorate. In addition to the fellowship, she says the dean, Dr. Robert Douglass, made it very clear he wanted her to stay with the school after completing her PhD. And she did, until retiring in 1996. "You talk about a gift dropping in your lap!"[65]

Dr. Herring became a full-time faculty member specializing in children's literature and school librarianship, but the school was still shorthanded, so she also was assigned reference and, later, cataloging instruction.

> **So I was spending every minute in the library getting acquainted with the reference materials and often skipped lunch because my class was at one o'clock and I was still downstairs in the library trying to get used to the—[laughs]—trying to get used to all those materials and get ready to teach.**[66]

Dr. Herring found that she really loved teaching cataloging—even though she had never actually been a cataloger in a library. However, her inexperience with the discipline of cataloging may have led her to a teaching style that profoundly influenced generations of students at UT. She describes her method as "mastery-based." Proctors would work with individual students until they mastered the particular cataloging assignment. Dr. Herring would not let a student fail: the student simply had to repeat the assignment until she got it right.

So Dr. Herring's initial career as a librarian came about in the checkout line at the grocery store because the superintendent needed a school librarian—and not a substitute teacher—and her career as a professor was due to the severe shortage of faculty. She never intended to be a school librarian and then she never intended to be anything but a school librarian. Generations of librarians in Texas have benefited from these twists of fate that led Dr. Herring to become a beloved teacher and mentor at the library school.

Dr. Mary Bushing began her professional life as a true vocation—she was a nun. Here is her story:

> **When I was eighteen, I went in the convent and I was a Benedictine nun for five years. And one of the things that happened in those days was that an educational plan was decided for each of the people who entered. Of course, you weren't involved in those decisions. It was based strictly on what they saw as your strengths and all of that. . . . I was one of those people who got good grades in math and science as well as in the humanities and other things. And they thought that I was going to be a great librarian, because I would know a little bit about everything.**[67]

The convent had decided that she was to earn her BA and then study at Rosary College—now Dominican University—to get an MLS and take advantage of her aptitude as a generalist. She was apprised of her "plan" by the sisters when she left the convent. The plan also included studying at Notre Dame for a doctorate in philosophy.

> **I never did get my doctorate in philosophy. I did get one in adult and higher education, but I married a philosopher ultimately, so I figure it is sort of the same thing. And I fulfilled their educational plans for me.**
>
> **When my children were getting to be of an age when I really had to go to work, I wanted to finish my BA and get a library degree. It never occurred to me not to. It seemed like I was born to be a librarian anyway. And besides that was the plan. . . . So I did in fact go to Rosary College and get my MLS.**[68]

At the end of her interview, Dr. Bushing sums up her career and her thoughts about the profession:

> **This is a fabulous way to earn a living. The salaries aren't great. You will never get rich, but it's a fabulous way to earn a living. There are so many paybacks. And you have a mind full of useless information that you can pull out at cocktail parties . . . interesting information you accumulate as a librarian.**
>
> **But you have to have a passion for what you are doing. You have to like people and you have to be someone who is comfortable with ambiguity.**
>
> **There are no right or wrong answers. If not finding the right answer paralyzes you, this isn't the job for you. You have got to be comfortable with ambiguity and you have to be willing to constantly change and adjust. And if change is hard for you, then you need to either get help to make it easier or find some other kind of work. . . . It is a wonderful job . . . whatever hat you wear.**[69]

I asked my cataloging colleague and friend, John Myers, if he was interested in interviewing any of his mentors. He had worked with Dorothy McGarry on several ALA committees and had always found her to be astute and congenial, but recently he had discovered a monograph of Seymour Lubetzky's lectures that had been compiled and edited by Ms. McGarry—and this piqued his interest in sitting down with her for an oral history interview. The three of us met in Boston for the 2010 ALA Midwinter Meeting.

Ms. McGarry is a retired physical sciences and technology librarian at UCLA. She received her library degree from that same school in 1971, though she began her library career much earlier. After finishing her bachelor's degree in 1949, she began work on a master's in library science in 1950. But family life interrupted her studies until she was able to return to the classroom in 1970.

She has always been interested in cataloging and mathematics, and she believes this was the reason she was hired for her first professional position:

> **I started working at UCLA as a paraprofessional in '68. And then I decided, "Well, this is silly, I should go to library school." . . . Before I went back I had taken a number of mathematics classes at San Fernando Valley State College. And that was one of the main reasons that I got my job at UCLA as librarian. When I was hired the woman in charge of the Engineering—Physical Sciences—whatever it was called at that time—Library hated to catalog mathematics books. And so she figured she could give me all the mathematics books, and that's why she hired me instead of the other person. So that's put me in good stead.**[70]

Our conversation, among three catalogers, focused on cataloging, especially because John and I were just in awe of Ms. McGarry's breadth of knowledge—and she had actually met Seymour Lubetzky. (We marveled at our degrees of separation by having her in the room with us.) Because she has worked on a very technical level since the early 1970s, she has implemented several new standards—which were just as disruptive as the current twenty-first-century cataloging challenges. She began working with AACR (Anglo-American Cataloging Rules) and then implemented AACR2 (Anglo-American Cataloging Rules, 2nd edition) in a card catalog. These records were retrospectively converted to MARC for the digital catalog and have been massaged in different ways to reflect advancing technologies in the computer age. And now these records are being converted to RDA (Resource Description and Access) standards with FRBR (Functional Requirements for Bibliographic Records) information possibly being incorporated as well. One of our questions was about the process of retrospective conversion—from the shelflist to MARC for online access. Here Ms. McGarry acknowledges that the process is ongoing. She continues to work on the project of converting her library's most specialized older works, although she retired several years ago:

> **Well, I might explain that right now I'm allowed to volunteer to do this because the administration can never be expected to hire someone to do this, so I'm working on cleaning up the database for both Science and Engineering libraries. And there are hundreds of serials that still have never been converted, and so I'm working at trying to convert them. Some have been converted locally but not tied with any OCLC record, so I've been trying to do that, but there are also hundreds and hundreds of monographs that have never been converted.**[71]

Several things are notable about this story of Ms. McGarry's volunteer work at the institution she retired from, but what impresses me most is that it exemplifies the way so many of us regard our jobs. The creation of this catalog has been her life's work, and it is important work because it is the tool that allows research librarians and scholars to access meaningful information. Librarianship is more than simply a job. It is a mission. And Ms. McGarry continues this mission even in retirement.

Ms. McGarry says that she comes in just part-time and might convert one hundred items a month—and clean up three to four hundred authority entries in the process. I asked her how far through the old shelflist she had progressed in this final sweep of retrospective conversion:

> **"M" . . . It's good for me, too, because it gives me a focus when I'm in Los Angeles. It gives me something to do and keeps me interested and functioning. And so—I appreciate that they let me come in and do that.[72]**

Library School Memories

All librarians matriculated at a graduate school and earned a master's degree in library science, information science, or some combination. This social memory of library school is the first professional memory of their careers.

Rita Auerbach remembers going to library school at Columbia University when computers were still a novelty. But she understood that they were going to be an important resource in the future, so she made sure to take the one computer class offered by her program—which happened to be scheduled at the same time as the only children's literature class. She never got to take that children's literature class, which is ironic because she has devoted her entire career to children's librarianship and even chaired the Caldecott Medal Selection Committee.

Ms. Auerbach was warned to not expect a great deal of intellectual rigor at library school. A friend of hers who was a library director told her that library school would be dull and full of tedious work but that she should persevere because being a librarian was very rewarding.

> **So I carried that advice with me to library school. And sure enough it wasn't enormously intellectually challenging, but they piled on an enormous amount of work, I think to prove that it was an intellectual challenge. And every time something wonderful would happen and I would enjoy it, I'd start to get nervous because if**

> **there was an inverse relationship between your reaction to library school and your love of the profession, I was afraid maybe I wouldn't love being a librarian!**
>
> **But it turns out I have. I've shared that advice with other people who've thought about dropping out of library school and inspired them to go on and they've thanked me afterwards. So I can't say this is true of all library schools, but I must say that I loved working as a librarian a whole lot more than I liked learning to be one.[73]**

Connie Corson studied at Columbia and graduated in 1962. She appreciated the library science theory taught in school but felt that many of the day-to-day skills required for running a library could only be picked up on the job. She has always recommended that potential librarians work at a library before or during master's degree work so they are equipped with both practical and theoretical skills when they graduate.

John Mitchell's time in library school was just at the cusp of MARC implementation. Because he was able to learn MARC and how to catalog in an electronic environment at Catholic University in Washington, D.C., he came to the Library of Congress as a new cataloger with a considerable advantage over most of the library's more senior staff.

Pat Tuohy attended the University of Texas and graduated in 1970. She had planned to be an academic librarian but shifted her focus to public libraries. When the interviewer asked what led her to make this decision in library school, she replied, without hesitation, "Cataloging. Let's be perfectly clear, it was cataloging."[74] In the first section of this chapter I quoted her story about Billie Grace Herring "giving" her a B in the basic cataloging class so that she could continue her studies, but the academic librarianship track required the advanced cataloging course. Ms. Tuohy says that when she told Dr. Herring that she was switching her focus to public libraries, Dr. Herring enthusiastically told her she was going to make a great public librarian and it was the right choice. And it was the right choice for Ms. Tuohy. She went on to work for the Austin Public

Library and then to inspire and counsel hundreds of her peers as the director of the Central Texas Library System.

Hatred of cataloging class is mentioned in more than just Ms. Tuohy's interview. Robert Gaines, Peggy Richwine, Karen Breen, Karlan Sick, and Richard Corson all professed a deep antipathy toward learning cataloging in library school. Mr. Gaines says it was his "least favorite class. Not that there's anything wrong with cataloging. . . ."[75] Ms. Richwine says her cataloging class was simply "a matter of endurance,"[76] which is ironic because she spent a great deal of her later career organizing materials. When Ms. Sick was asked about her least favorite class, she replied, "Oh, I suppose cataloging—like everybody."[77] Ms. Breen was more emphatic about it: "Oh yeah, cataloging. No question. Oy!"[78]

Though cataloging class memories are remarkably hostile, librarians who survived cataloging class and went on to become catalogers look back fondly to those library school memories and worry that library schools are abdicating their responsibilities in order to make cataloging more palatable. Dorothy McGarry states the following (being interviewed by two other catalogers, John Myers and myself):

> **It's harder to learn to catalog. I think you have to have an education in cataloging, in library school, so you can be trained to catalog on the job. And, I think you can't do away with the education, I think it's important not to have just someone who's going to teach you, "Follow the rules and type this catalog card" or whatever it used to be. You have to have somebody who—who talked about what's there at the background, ah, what some of the options had been, and why they chose the option they did when they made the rules, this type of thing. . . .**
>
> **Not everyone makes a good cataloger, but I think everyone needs cataloging in library school if they're going to be a good reference librarian, or are going to be a good, um, ah, selector, selection, whatever, even administrators need to know something**

about cataloging to know what's reasonable to expect from the catalogers.

One thing, you have to have a good teacher. Library schools not only have to offer the course, and should require the course, but they have to have a good teacher. Because if someone takes—it's like math in a way—if you take the course and don't have a good teacher, you're not really going to come out of it comprehending what's there.[79]

The dislike—or terror—of cataloging is so prevalent that it is a cliché. In the next chapter we examine the use of cliché and stereotype within the oral history interviews.

NOTES

1. Peggy Richwine, interview by Kacy Allgood, August 27, 2008, video recording, transcript, A. Arro Smith "Capturing Our Stories" Oral Histories Program, 2005-2012 97/1/70, American Library Association Archives at the University of Illinois, Urbana-Champaign, 10:03.
2. Karen Breen, interview by Kristy Raffensberger, June 4, 2008, audio recording, transcript, A. Arro Smith "Capturing Our Stories" Oral Histories Program, 2005-2012 97/1/70, American Library Association Archives at the University of Illinois, Urbana-Champaign, 01:33.
3. Ibid., 00:44.
4. Bill Mears, interview by Stephanie Langenkamp and Arro Smith, February 29, 2007, video recording, transcript, A. Arro Smith "Capturing Our Stories" Oral Histories Program, 2005-2012 97/1/70, American Library Association Archives at the University of Illinois, Urbana-Champaign, 09:03.
5. Ibid., 06:09.
6. Connie (Cornelia) Corson, interview by Jane Brodsky Fitzpatrick, August 3, 2009, audio recording, transcript, A. Arro Smith "Capturing Our Stories" Oral Histories Program, 2005-2012 97/1/70, American Library Association Archives at the University of Illinois, Urbana-Champaign, 05:17.
7. Ibid., 02:51.
8. Ibid., 18:54.

9. Richard Corson, interview by Jane Brodsky Fitzpatrick, July 17, 2009, audio recording, transcript, A. Arro Smith "Capturing Our Stories" Oral Histories Program, 2005-2012 97/1/70, American Library Association Archives at the University of Illinois, Urbana-Champaign, 01:39.
10. Ibid., 03:49.
11. Valerie Feinman, interview by Sarah Albert, June 29, 2008, video recording, transcript, A. Arro Smith "Capturing Our Stories" Oral Histories Program, 2005-2012 97/1/70, American Library Association Archives at the University of Illinois, Urbana-Champaign, 07:00.
12. Ibid., 12:18.
13. Ibid., 15:29.
14. Richwine, 23:22.
15. Nancy Clark Fogarty, interview by Anne Marie Taber, August 20, 2008, video recording, transcript, A. Arro Smith "Capturing Our Stories" Oral Histories Program, 2005-2012 97/1/70, American Library Association Archives at the University of Illinois, Urbana-Champaign, 03:37.
16. Ibid., 02:56.
17. Rita Auerbach, interview by Kristy Raffensberger, June 11, 2008, audio recording, transcript, A. Arro Smith "Capturing Our Stories" Oral Histories Program, 2005-2012 97/1/70, American Library Association Archives at the University of Illinois, Urbana-Champaign, 03:21.
18. Ibid., 02:59.
19. Ibid., 03:57.
20. Jennifer John Patterson, interview by Jennifer Jones, November 12, 2008, video recording, transcript, A. Arro Smith "Capturing Our Stories" Oral Histories Program, 2005-2012 97/1/70, American Library Association Archives at the University of Illinois, Urbana-Champaign, 04:53.
21. Jaye McLaughlin, interview by A. Arro Smith, April 16, 2011, video recording, transcript, A. Arro Smith "Capturing Our Stories" Oral Histories Program, 2005-2012 97/1/70, American Library Association Archives at the University of Illinois, Urbana-Champaign, 00:38.
22. Ibid., 11:52.
23. Ibid., 19:59.
24. Diana Collins, interview by Jessica Kirkland, November 16, 2008, video

recording, transcript, A. Arro Smith "Capturing Our Stories" Oral Histories Program, 2005-2012 97/1/70, American Library Association Archives at the University of Illinois, Urbana-Champaign, 35:37.

25. Ibid., 31:20.

26. Ibid., 32:57.

27. Ibid., 51:11.

28. Jeannette Larson, interview by Janssen Bradshaw, Allison Steeger, Kimberley Francisco, and Timothy Arnold, November 15, 2008, video recording, transcript, A. Arro Smith "Capturing Our Stories" Oral Histories Program, 2005-2012 97/1/70, American Library Association Archives at the University of Illinois, Urbana-Champaign, 07:56.

29. Ibid., 24:56.

30. Ibid., 31:14.

31. Kenneth Yamashita, interview by A. Arro Smith, June 28, 2010, video recording, transcript, A. Arro Smith "Capturing Our Stories" Oral Histories Program, 2005-2012 97/1/70, American Library Association Archives at the University of Illinois, Urbana-Champaign, 10:24.

32. Ibid., 07:10.

33. Ibid., 04:42.

34. Ibid., 34:11.

35. Kathy Kaya, interview by Mary Bushing, June 6, 2010, video recording, transcript, A. Arro Smith "Capturing Our Stories" Oral Histories Program, 2005-2012 97/1/70, American Library Association Archives at the University of Illinois, Urbana-Champaign, 18:14.

36. Sheila Ross Henderson, interview by Cathy Prazak, April 15, 2010, video recording, transcript, A. Arro Smith "Capturing Our Stories" Oral Histories Program, 2005-2012 97/1/70, American Library Association Archives at the University of Illinois, Urbana-Champaign, 42:57.

37. Ibid., 09:55.

38. Ibid., 10:09.

39. Ibid., 21:22.

40. Robert Gaines, interview by Anne Marie Taber, August 15, 2008, video recording, transcript, A. Arro Smith "Capturing Our Stories" Oral Histories

Program, 2005-2012 97/1/70, American Library Association Archives at the University of Illinois, Urbana-Champaign, 05:14.

41. Ibid., 25:38.

42. Ibid., 23:30.

43. Sandy (Sanford) Berman, interview by Tina Gross, August 18, 2012, video recording, transcript, A. Arro Smith "Capturing Our Stories" Oral Histories Program, 2005-2012 97/1/70, American Library Association Archives at the University of Illinois, Urbana-Champaign, 31:18.

44. Ibid., 61:03.

45. Ibid., 99:16.

46. Micki Freeny, interview by A. Arro Smith, July 10, 2009, video recording, transcript, A. Arro Smith "Capturing Our Stories" Oral Histories Program, 2005-2012 97/1/70, American Library Association Archives at the University of Illinois, Urbana-Champaign, 01:29.

47. Ibid., 03:02.

48. Andrew Hansen, interview by A. Arro Smith, July 13, 2009, video recording, transcript, A. Arro Smith "Capturing Our Stories" Oral Histories Program, 2005-2012 97/1/70, American Library Association Archives at the University of Illinois, Urbana-Champaign, 03:01.

49. Ibid., 04:34.

50. Ibid., 45:23.

51. Gail Hueting, interview by Kathryn La Barre, April 29, 2011, video recording, transcript, A. Arro Smith "Capturing Our Stories" Oral Histories Program, 2005-2012 97/1/70, American Library Association Archives at the University of Illinois, Urbana-Champaign, 01:37.

52. Ibid., 36:07.

53. Arlene Luster, interview by A. Arro Smith, July 11, 2009, video recording, transcript, A. Arro Smith "Capturing Our Stories" Oral Histories Program, 2005-2012 97/1/70, American Library Association Archives at the University of Illinois, Urbana-Champaign, 11:37.

54. Irene Hoadley, interview by Joan Heath and A. Arro Smith, April 27, 2010, video recording, transcript, A. Arro Smith "Capturing Our Stories" Oral Histories Program, 2005-2012 97/1/70, American Library Association Archives at the University of Illinois, Urbana-Champaign, 01:34.

55. Ibid., 06:14.
56. Sarah Ann Long, interview by Ninfa Trejo, June 27, 2008, video recording, transcript, A. Arro Smith "Capturing Our Stories" Oral Histories Program, 2005-2012 97/1/70, American Library Association Archives at the University of Illinois, Urbana-Champaign, 10:29.
57. Ibid., 32:38.
58. Ninfa Trejo, interview by Sarah Ann Long, June 27, 2008, video recording, transcript, A. Arro Smith "Capturing Our Stories" Oral Histories Program, 2005-2012 97/1/70, American Library Association Archives at the University of Illinois, Urbana-Champaign, 00:41.
59. Ibid., 02:15.
60. Patricia Tuohy, interview by Jessica Kirkland, June 17, 2009, video recording, transcript, A. Arro Smith "Capturing Our Stories" Oral Histories Program, 2005-2012 97/1/70, American Library Association Archives at the University of Illinois, Urbana-Champaign, 01:09.
61. Ibid., 05:34.
62. Ibid., 03:15.
63. Ibid.
64. Billie Grace Herring, interview by Michael McCombs, October 21, 2011, video recording, transcript, A. Arro Smith "Capturing Our Stories" Oral Histories Program, 2005-2012 97/1/70, American Library Association Archives at the University of Illinois, Urbana-Champaign, 04:40.
65. Ibid., 14:17.
66. Ibid., 13:26.
67. Mary Bushing, interview by Kathy Kaya, June 6, 2010, video recording, transcript, A. Arro Smith "Capturing Our Stories" Oral Histories Program, 2005-2012 97/1/70, American Library Association Archives at the University of Illinois, Urbana-Champaign, 02:19.
68. Ibid.
69. Ibid., 46:31.
70. Dorothy McGarry, interview by John Myers and A. Arro Smith, January 15, 2010, video recording, transcript, A. Arro Smith "Capturing Our Stories" Oral Histories Program, 2005-2012 97/1/70, American Library Association Archives at the University of Illinois, Urbana-Champaign, 10:38.

71. Ibid., 32:04.
72. Ibid., 41:59.
73. Auerbach, 04:32.
74. Tuohy, 03:00.
75. Gaines, 09:09.
76. Richwine, 16:03.
77. Karlan Sick, interview by Kristy Raffensberger, May 19, 2008, audio recording, transcript, A. Arro Smith "Capturing Our Stories" Oral Histories Program, 2005-2012 97/1/70, American Library Association Archives at the University of Illinois, Urbana-Champaign, 04:40.
78. Breen, 06:06.
79. McGarry, 58:32.

Chapter 2

CLICHÉ AND STEREOTYPE

IN EACH CASE WHERE THE INTERVIEWEES MENTION DISLIKING their cataloging class in library school, it is clear by the timbre of their remarks that they assume almost everyone would agree with them. In fact, all the interviewers can be heard murmuring in agreement—and sometimes laughing. The dislike of cataloging (at least among non-catalogers) is a library cliché. The following two sections examine elements of the social memory that employ cliché and include selections from the interviews that discuss stereotypes within and outside the profession.

Use of Cliché

Cataloging and catalogers are the subjects of several clichés in the social memory of librarianship. John Mitchell, a retired cataloger for the Library of Congress, first uses cliché to distinguish himself from the stereotype of most catalogers by saying that, contrary to the "normal Myers-Briggs cataloger," he is actually gregarious and very outgoing.[1] But later in the interview he returns to the subject with another cliché, saying that a good cataloger has a very focused attention to detail and that "we lose sight of the forest for the individual tree sometimes in cataloging."[2] He goes on to say that catalogers pay a great deal of attention to rules. They want to follow rules, and this propensity "may be sometimes an enigma to our colleagues."[3]

Janet Swan Hill, also a cataloger, employs the same cliché about technical services staff not seeing the forest for the trees, but she argues for the opposite of the stereotype. She believes it is the public services staff who do see the individual trees, because each scenario is unique. Ms. Hill argues that the catalogers are looking for patterns—so they can apply agreed-upon rules based on those patterns:

> **Catalogers are very often accused of not seeing the forest for the trees. In my experience catalogers see the forest. . . . Public services people see only each individual tree. They deal with this tree as a one-off, and then there is another tree and they deal with it. Catalogers look at a problem and say what are—what is the class of things to which this belongs? What precedents will I set by making this decision? What forest does it grow in? If I plant this tree here, how will that influence everything else? So I think that it is a character trait—that may not be terribly common among people—to look at things in terms of patterns. Catalogers are pattern seekers.**[4]

She continues, saying that catalogers are detail-oriented because they must find the details that matter and apply cataloging and classification rules so the library works efficiently. And then the public services staff can address the individual trees daily because the forest is well organized by the technical services staff.

Bill Mears echoes this cliché about catalogers when he describes how he interviews and hires people. He tries to assess their people skills during an interview, regardless of their other qualifications. Dr. Mears says the only reason he has ever had to fire someone in his forty years of experience is that the person could not work well with others—whether coworkers or patrons. He could train or coach a poorly performing librarian to find an effective place within his organization, but he could never change an employee's basic people skills no matter how hard he tried. He uses cliché at the end of this passage when he states, "And that even applies to the librarians that are in tech services."[5]

Janet Swan Hill invokes the cliché of the monkish cataloger using the technical services department as a retreat from the real world. She states, "It's not a matter of sitting there all by yourself transcribing things like a monk . . . because it is no retreat."[6]

Jeannette Larson makes a similar offhand comment about catalogers, also in reference to how everyone working at the library needs to possess interpersonal skills—even in technical services. She refers to catalogers as people who typically do not want to be in front of everybody or who do not want to deal with kids, but she also self-references the comment, calling it a stereotype that might not be wholly accurate.[7]

Clichés are not just used about catalogers but applied generally to the entire profession within the social memory. When Dr. Yamashita is discussing his brief career as a representative for an integrated library systems vendor, he mentions that he was not a very good salesman. In this interview it is the interviewer (me) who employs the cliché by saying "most librarians aren't good salesmen."[8]

Dr. Dale Ricklefs uses a similar cliché when talking about why she was hired by the city manager of Round Rock, Texas:

> **Even though the library skills were needed, he had interviewed many librarians who were very much the librarian or librarian's librarian. He was looking for someone who could manage to go with the flow when necessary—which is what happens in politics.**[9]

The stereotype invoked by this cliché is that most librarians may not possess the interpersonal skills to work well within a contentious political atmosphere.

When Jennifer John Patterson gives some advice to new professionals at the conclusion of her interview, she employs a subtle cliché also decrying the tendency of librarians to be introverted:

> **Work on believing in yourself, work on your social skills, work on knowing how to be charming and interesting to other people. You know, all of the same things that anyone else needs to succeed in life, we need to succeed in life. It's not a place to hide, it's not a place to rest, it is challenging.**[10]

Kathy Kaya echoes this cliché when she relates her own interpersonal metamorphosis. When she joined the faculty of Montana State University, she realized she needed to push beyond her comfort zone and speak out rather than wait for her turn. She reports that this skill was very difficult for her to learn.[11]

Jaye McLaughlin, a children's librarian for her entire career, tells a story about visiting an academic library. Her use of cliché is also subtle but telling:

> **The librarian that was there helping with students looked very at ease with what he was doing and very approachable. And so, you know, I think those traits are something that we really need to emphasize because we really aren't the "shushing" librarians anymore.**[12]

The implication is that librarians are usually not "at ease" when working with the public, a trait that must be compensated for.

The stereotype about shy librarians may be a legacy of gender in the history of librarianship. Pat Tuohy invokes this cliché when she explains to her interviewer how women's clubs were pivotal in the genesis of many small Texas public libraries:

> **In my experience, it's the women of the community, usually better educated, or just they love to read. They don't have to be better educated, but they have a love of reading and education and a real respect for it. And they were the impetus to start the library. And I have seen this in all of these libraries that have started, it's mainly women that are doing this. And there are men involved—don't get me wrong, there are energetic male volunteers—but it is heavily women and it's women in the community who have standing.**
>
> **Whether they're newcomers to the community or they're the old grandes dames, or the daughters of the old grandes dames, they have standing and they're doing this for their community. They're doing this for Moody [Texas] or Mart [Texas] or whatever community they're in to make it better. . . .**
>
> **And this is an established pattern for public library development. It goes back to the women's clubs—the Texas Federation of Women's Clubs. The old-time libraries, like Llano [Texas], were established by the Literary Guild or the Ladies of Fortnightly Club. The Fortnightly Club in Brenham, Texas, is over one hundred years old and they established a public library. And that could have been a bookshelf in the county courthouse or in the basement, but they were the impetus to start a library. And this is like 18-something, '90 or 1901.**
>
> **So—and many of these women's clubs, they were literary societies, they read books and talked about them. They cared about the education in the community and they wanted a library. And these had to be the better educated, more affluent members of that community.**[13]

Peggy Richwine was a science librarian at a university. At one point her interviewer asks how Ms. Richwine feels about taking the word *library* out of the name of her alma mater's degree program—and that of many other library and information science schools. Ms. Richwine replies by discussing a tangential cliché: that any discipline that "has science in its name is not a real science." She does not have a particularly strong opinion about the word *library*, but she has always felt uncomfortable with the word *science* because of the cliché among her peers within the hard sciences. Ms. Richwine would be more comfortable calling the profession "information management" because that is what she has done. She reminds the interviewer that her career began with managing only print materials. Her career has been an arc from working with print to working almost exclusively with electronic materials. She believes using the term *information management* is a more accurate description of the discipline because it lacks the print-based connotation of *library* and the derisive cliché of *science*.[14]

Jeannette Larson compares librarianship to the Mafia:

> **And it's a little bit like the Mafia. They never let you out, you're never—they pull you back. Because I still get calls, you know—I left the state library thirteen years ago, and I still get calls saying, "institutional memory, how did we get started doing such and such, do you remember why we made this decision and we did this," you know?**
>
> **And I also think that's one of the wonderful things about working in libraries and with other librarians—is that we do talk to each other and we do stay. You're never sort of not a librarian anymore.**[15]

Karlan Sick echoes Ms. Larson's comment about never not being a librarian. She says she has to "bite her tongue" not to recommend books to people when she is shopping in a bookstore.

Karen Breen's interview includes several uses of cliché. She refers to behaviors that she assumes all librarians share. From the tenor of her comments, it is clear that these are elements of her story she believes are part of the social memory of the profession. The first instance involves her postretirement career as a children's bookstore owner. She says, "I bought a children's bookstore—every children's librarian wants to do it for themselves, you understand." She reports that after three and a half years she sold the store "and got that out of my system."[16] In another offhand comment, she talks about visiting other libraries when traveling. She rhetorically asks her interviewer, "Don't we all go to every library that we can look at?"[17] Both of these clichéd references assume the interviewer's familiarity with a shared vocabulary of memory.

Stereotype and Cliché

Stereotype and cliché are closely related and are often used as synonyms. But for this study the terms have been cleaved from each other in order to explore two separate but related facets of the social memory. The term *stereotype* is used when the interviewee discusses the subject of library stereotypes. The term *cliché* is used when a subject employs a library stereotype during the interview as shorthand for an aspect of the social memory without actually discussing the term's resonance as a stereotype.

The corpus of interviews documents specific stereotypes that are part of the social memory within the profession, but especially from outside the profession. First, a review of the definition of *stereotype:* in *Stereotype and Status: Librarians in the United States,* Pauline Wilson discusses the origin of the term as argot from the early days of the printing press. Printing with movable type involved casting a metal plate that was used to make duplicate inked images on paper. This metal plate was called a *stereotype.* The term's use in the social sciences dates from the 1920s to refer to a synecdoche of traits that are perceived to be repeated throughout a culture.[18]

Several of the interviewees discuss the most popular image of librarianship: the meek female—perhaps spinster—who completely lacks social charm and is primarily concerned with protecting the library collection from human depredations. And when they discuss this stereotype they almost always identify in opposition to the stereotype, unless they are also employing self-deprecating humor.

When librarians use a cliché—as opposed to discussing the stereotype—they are often referring to the very same personality traits that popular culture has assigned to the profession while using the cliché to identify themselves in opposition or as a means of criticizing their peers. The most startling repeated use of cliché found in the *Stories* interviews involves non-catalogers speaking about the technical services staff members or about their hatred of cataloging classes in library school. This stereotype is earned by catalogers because cataloging is perceived as a difficult and tedious aspect of librarianship. I can attest that for someone without a generous aptitude for organization, cataloging class may be the most difficult trial of library school.[19] Catalogers and technical services staff members do, indeed, stay out of the public eye at many libraries, so they may very well conform to the stereotype.

Catalogers themselves like to talk about their particular skills and personality traits in the *Stories* interviews. Two different catalogers use virtually the same cliché—though one claims that catalogers often "don't see the forest for the trees,"[20] and the other states that catalogers do see the forest because they are able to organize the entire body of knowledge whereas public services staff cannot see the forest because they must be concerned with each individual tree.[21]

What the cliché signals when depicting catalogers is a cleavage between the public services staff and the technical services staff—this is the explicit message. The implicit message is that the two librarians are different—that different aptitudes are required for each position.

Discussing the Stereotype

The difference between using a cliché and discussing a stereotype is subtle but important. Oral history interviews are self-reflective, by their very nature. In addition to using cliché to tell their stories, many of the interviewees address the stereotypes that have been part of their professional lives. These stereotypes can be divided into two main groups: those from within the profession and those from without.

STEREOTYPES WITHIN THE PROFESSION

One such stereotype within the profession is a hierarchy of perceived prestige. Connie Corson was anxious about the perception that she was stepping down the ladder of librarian prestige by taking a job as a school librarian after a career as a librarian at the Museum of Modern Art and then at a university. She had never even considered being a school librarian, but she was asked to serve on the selection committee at a private girls' school in New York City that needed to hire a new librarian. After touring the campus and talking with some of the teachers and the headmaster, she came home and announced to her husband—also an academic librarian—that she was embarrassed to be thinking that she might want the job. She was worried that after she had spent years building a prestigious career as an academic librarian, people would feel that she was "stepping down" to be a children's librarian or a school librarian. She did take the position—much to the surprise of the administrators who had only asked her to serve on the search committee—and never regretted the decision.[22]

Later, in the section about library funding challenges, Jeannette Larson alludes to a stereotype about city managers working with public libraries. She refers to the following as "a joke" within the profession: that the library is a footnote in the annual budget until the city manager has a child attending storytime. She wishes there were more consistent ways to attract the attention of funding authorities than simply waiting for them to have toddlers.[23]

Janet Swan Hill laments the position of technical services within the perceived library hierarchy, especially within LIS graduate education:

> **When you are a minority, it is easy to be overlooked and to have the rest of the faculty in the library school—in the LIS programs—**

> **not quite understand why it is important to what you are doing and emphasizing other [library subdisciplines]. . . . Those people advise students and they say, "There's no future in cataloging. Why would you want to do that?"—with that kind of attitude—or they sneer at it—anecdotally they sneer at it—or make jokes at the expense of information organization. Well, of course people aren't going to come into the field.**
>
> **Also, we don't tend to attract into the field from many of the subject disciplines that would have a special affinity for cataloging—like music or philosophy or mathematics. If all you get is English and history majors, you are going to get English and history majors and they are not as likely to be interested in cataloging as somebody who took Latin. . . . So you start with—you have self-selected out most of the people who might be drawn to cataloging, and then you subject them to an LIS program in which cataloging and other related activities are not stressed and may even be made a joke of.**[24]

Sandy Berman concurs with Ms. Hill about the state of cataloging within our profession:

> **I lament what I think is truly the decline of cataloging. . . . That there are fewer catalogers and there is less impetus or encouragement—and less encouragement to, like, really ply their trade and exercise their own creativity and insight in actually working, like, with a new piece of material coming through: "How can I make it more accessible, more useful to the people who are going to come in and use the catalog?"**[25]

STEREOTYPES OUTSIDE THE PROFESSION

Librarians in the United States live with a powerful stereotype. The cliché that librarians are meek, frumpy, unmarried women with their hair in

FIGURE 1. Librarian from *The Philadelphia Story*

a bun, half-eye glasses perched on their nose, and wearing sensible shoes while patrolling the library stacks and shushing patrons is so pervasive in twentieth-century culture that it really needs no documentation; however, please indulge me with my personal favorite films involving librarians. In the first example, a librarian has only a fleeting role, but both demonstrate the power of the stereotype.

In *The Philadelphia Story,* Jimmy Stewart plays a newspaper reporter who visits the local library to research the family of an heiress (played by Katharine Hepburn) whom he has been sent to investigate. The librarian asks him, "What is thee wish?" Stewart does a double take at the anachronistic idiom and asks her to repeat it—just to make sure he has heard her correctly. In deference to the librarian's grammar, and without guile, he asks, "Dost thou have a washroom?" and then, "Thank thee."[26] In addition to speaking straight from the King James Bible, the librarian is efficient yet brittle and can only be described as "mousey." Her final words in the scene are "Shush, shush" (figure 1).

FIGURE 2. Librarians in *Desk Set*

In *Desk Set*, librarian Katharine Hepburn and her crew of research assistants work both sides of the stereotype as they fact-check for a broadcasting company and fight being replaced by the new "electronic brain"—a computer named ENIAC. The librarian and the research assistants are smart, but they are also demurely sexy and funny (figure 2). In addition to being able to quote challenging and obscure passages from Longfellow, they are concerned with the latest fashions from Gimbels. Hepburn's character is able to rattle off the following lines from Longfellow's *The Song of Hiawatha* from memory: "By the shores of Gitche Gumee, / By the shining Big-Sea-Water, / Stood the wigwam of Nokomis, / Daughter of the Moon, Nokomis. / Dark behind it rose the forest, / Rose the black and gloomy pine-trees, / Rose the firs with cones upon them; / Bright before it beat the water, / Beat the clear and sunny water, / Beat the shining Big-Sea-Water." It is a tour-de-force performance—what every librarian aspires to be.[27]

The picture is a romantic comedy, and Hepburn ultimately chooses the affections of Spencer Tracy over those of Gig Young. But the comedy of the picture is contingent on the viewer's notions of the librarian stereotype and on the fact that the cliché normally does not allow for librarians to be seen in a romantic role. Both the anonymous librarian in *The Philadelphia Story* and Hepburn in *Desk Set* wear their hair in a bun (see figures 1 and 2).

Librarians have long fought this stereotype.[28] However, I find that many of the interview subjects refer to the stereotype or use librarian clichés to discuss their careers and their self-perceptions or to place themselves within the larger community of librarianship. By acknowledging the stereotype, librarians use the cliché as a synecdoche for their personalities and the history of the profession. They also use it to define how they are different from society's perception of the profession.

A persistent stereotype from outside the profession is that everyone who works at the library is a librarian. Many of the interview subjects refer to fighting this stereotype. Kent Middleton blames the error on the profession not properly educating the public about itself. He believes that at least 90 percent of the public thinks that circulation clerks are librarians, even though only a high school degree is required for the position at his institution. Peggy Richwine laments the fact that most people have no idea librarians hold master's degrees—and often a second master's degree in their discipline of bibliographic specialization if they are academic librarians. And to be a really capable librarian "requires a great deal of skill and intelligence and effort. I think people have no idea what is required of being a librarian. Training and experience all come together to make your role as a librarian much more valuable."[29]

In the first chapter, on becoming a librarian, Rita Auerbach says that librarianship was not her first career choice: "No, and it was my last choice of a job. I was sure that librarians sat around and waited for people to ask where the bathroom was, and that didn't seem like an intellectually stimulating way of life."[30] In this instance, she is referring to her own perception of the stereotype prior to becoming a librarian. Later in the interview, she refers to the stereotype when discussing others' perceptions of her career:

> **People would come up to me and say, "Oh, I'd love to have your job. I love to read, I could sit around all day and read." And maybe there's a subset of people who don't realize that the people checking the books out are not trained librarians.**[31]

In chapter 1, Arlene Luster shared her inspiration for pursuing a career as a librarian: the little rubber stamp on the end of the pencil that she witnessed a clerk using in her childhood library. She later discusses why she always insisted that the desk for the reference librarian was clearly separate from the circulation activities. This placement was to provide a visual cue to the patron that there is a difference between the positions. Dr. Luster chuckles when remembering her initial rubber stamp inspiration to become a librarian—because she now realizes that the person was probably not a librarian but a clerk.[32]

But by far the most common stereotype involves the "shushing librarian." As with my reference to *The Philadelphia Story*, Robert Gaines refers to a Jimmy Stewart motion picture in his interview:

> **There certainly have been social stereotypes over the years. In the early part of my career—I guess everyone remembers the *It's a Wonderful Life* stereotype of the poor lady being relegated to opening the library—the famous Jimmy Stewart film which we see many, many times every Christmas. So there was the stereotype that most librarians were female, and rather dowdy and saying "shh" all the time rather than being terribly helpful.**
>
> **I think that stereotype was always mistaken, and always was a mistake. It was always just a stereotype. Because I started using libraries, as I said, in 1949. I joined—I got a card—I got my card to access the Nashville Public Library—and I always found librarians to be professional and helpful and knowledgeable. . . . I actually never heard a librarian go "shh" in my entire life.**[33]

Kenneth Yamashita also specifically refers to the stereotype of "middle-aged Caucasian female with a bun who has her hand up here [shushing]."[34] He echoes Mr. Gaines's comment that a good librarian is the exact opposite of the common stereotype—that the effective librarian is not someone who wants to sit in the background and read a book, but, rather, someone who is "passionate about public service and has good communication skills . . . more service-oriented than book-oriented."[35]

Many of the interviewees refer to this stereotype when discussing the type of person that makes a good librarian. Irene Hoadley says of academic librarianship that, contrary to the stereotype, "you didn't want somebody that was going to come and wants to sit in a little corner. And that's what people's concepts of libraries were at that point in time. Maybe it is still for some people, I don't know."[36] Karen Breen agrees, saying about children's librarianship, "Let's make sure they know all of what this job is. It's not enough just to think that, 'I like children's books and I'm here holed up in this corner.'"[37]

Some librarians even celebrate their nonconformity to the stereotype. Jennifer John Patterson recalls the horror that her first supervisor expressed when she attempted to execute her first database search. She had been tasked with finding current periodical articles on calcium, but she had not understood the necessity of limiting the search string. She returned with a fat stack of dot-matrix printouts that were basically useless and had been invoiced per citation. She says, "It's very hard for me to be as orderly and methodical as a librarian is normally expected to be."[38] She found her calling involved library programming, motivating her peers, and consulting—professional library work outside the scope of the stereotypical librarian.

Jeannette Larson also identifies in opposition to the stereotype. When discussing the modern library, she points out that it is not necessarily a quiet place anymore. And that the librarians are often the loudest people in the building. She celebrates the fact that contemporary libraries do not fit the stereotype:

> **They've become much more open and airy. And, you know, probably the greatest change—and again, this is kind of stereotypical—is that we're no longer the quiet places. In fact we're . . . bustling,**

> **busy places—not quiet, scholarly hideaways where everyone is sitting around reading. Now you've got conversations going, you've got machines clicking, you've got headphones that somebody's got up too loud, and they're busy, bustling places.**[39]

Mary Bushing warns that it is not an unstressful career:

> **This isn't a place where there is no stress. This isn't a place where you can retire from the world. . . . There is this—still—this underlying myth that somehow library work is—is kind of lovely.**
>
> **Library work is exciting, but I wouldn't describe it as lovely. So I guess, first of all, to understand that this is work that is challenging. Secondly, that this is work about relationship—relationships with the people who use the library, relationships with the people who fund the library, relationships with your colleagues. If you don't like people, think about a different job. This isn't the job for you.**
>
> **We have fewer and fewer backroom jobs where we can hide people who don't want to be interrupted in their work. This job is all about interruptions. No matter what you do. I mean, whether you are an administrator, whether you are a systems person, a reference or information person, even technical services, whatever you are doing, this job is about interruptions because it is a service job and that means response.**[40]

Karen Breen uses the word *defensive* about describing—or defending—what librarians actually do. She describes the stereotype as "the quiet nerd in the corner." Like Ms. Richwine, she has felt a lifelong enmity toward the stereotype and wishes the public could comprehend the amount of training and discipline required to be an effective librarian.[41]

If the stereotype of librarians invokes an image of a shy spinster more concerned with protecting the contents of her library than providing access to the materials, then the social memory of librarianship is precisely the opposite.

NOTES

1. John Mitchell, interview by A. Arro Smith, June 27, 2010, video recording, transcript, A. Arro Smith "Capturing Our Stories" Oral Histories Program, 2005-2012 97/1/70, American Library Association Archives at the University of Illinois, Urbana-Champaign, 12:44.
2. Ibid., 16:50.
3. Ibid., 12:37.
4. Janet Swan Hill, interview by A. Arro Smith, June 26, 2010, video recording, transcript, A. Arro Smith "Capturing Our Stories" Oral Histories Program, 2005-2012 97/1/70, American Library Association Archives at the University of Illinois, Urbana-Champaign, 21:37.
5. Bill Mears, interview by Stephanie Langenkamp and A. Arro Smith, February 29, 2007, video recording, transcript, A. Arro Smith "Capturing Our Stories" Oral Histories Program, 2005-2012 97/1/70, American Library Association Archives at the University of Illinois, Urbana-Champaign, 29:12.
6. Hill, 51:15.
7. Jeannette Larson, interview by Janssen Bradshaw, Allison Steeger, Kimberley Francisco, and Timothy Arnold, November 15, 2008, video recording, transcript, A. Arro Smith "Capturing Our Stories" Oral Histories Program, 2005-2012 97/1/70, American Library Association Archives at the University of Illinois, Urbana-Champaign, 02:51.
8. Kenneth Yamashita, interview by A. Arro Smith, June 28, 2010, video recording, transcript, A. Arro Smith "Capturing Our Stories" Oral Histories Program, 2005-2012 97/1/70, American Library Association Archives at the University of Illinois, Urbana-Champaign, 14:32.
9. Dale Ricklefs, interview by A. Arro Smith, Stephanie Langenkamp, and Pat Tuohy, April 8, 2011, video recording, transcript, A. Arro Smith "Capturing Our Stories" Oral Histories Program, 2005-2012 97/1/70, American Library Association Archives at the University of Illinois, Urbana-Champaign, 11:06.
10. Jennifer John Patterson, interview by Jennifer Jones, November 12, 2008, video recording, transcript, A. Arro Smith "Capturing Our Stories" Oral Histories Program, 2005-2012 97/1/70, American Library Association Archives at the University of Illinois, Urbana-Champaign, 45:59.

11. Kathy Kaya, interview by Mary Bushing, June 6, 2010, video recording, transcript, A. Arro Smith "Capturing Our Stories" Oral Histories Program, 2005-2012 97/1/70, American Library Association Archives at the University of Illinois, Urbana-Champaign, 05:19.
12. Jaye McLaughlin, interview by A. Arro Smith, April 16, 2011, video recording, transcript, A. Arro Smith "Capturing Our Stories" Oral Histories Program, 2005-2012 97/1/70, American Library Association Archives at the University of Illinois, Urbana-Champaign, 27:04.
13. Patricia Tuohy, interview by Jessica Kirkland, June 17, 2009, video recording, transcript, A. Arro Smith "Capturing Our Stories" Oral Histories Program, 2005-2012 97/1/70, American Library Association Archives at the University of Illinois, Urbana-Champaign, 41:54.
14. Richwine, 18:51.
15. Larson, 53:58.
16. Karen Breen, interview by Kristy Raffensberger, June 4, 2008, audio recording, transcript, A. Arro Smith "Capturing Our Stories" Oral Histories Program, 2005-2012 97/1/70, American Library Association Archives at the University of Illinois, Urbana-Champaign, 17:37.
17. Ibid., 27:52.
18. Pauline Wilson, *Stereotype and Status: Librarians in the United States* (Westport, CT: Greenwood Press, 1982).
19. A. Arro Smith, "Cataloging Heresy," in *Radical Cataloging: Essays at the Front*, K. R. Roberto, Editor (Jefferson, NC: McFarland, 2008).
20. Mitchell, 16:51.
21. Hill, 24:59.
22. Connie (Cornelia) Corson, interview by Jane Brodsky Fitzpatrick, August 3, 2009, audio recording, transcript, A. Arro Smith "Capturing Our Stories" Oral Histories Program, 2005-2012 97/1/70, American Library Association Archives at the University of Illinois, Urbana-Champaign, 27:44.
23. Larson, 19:15.
24. Hill, 41:50.
25. Sandy (Sanford) Berman, interview by Tina Gross, August 18, 2012, video recording, transcript, A. Arro Smith "Capturing Our Stories" Oral Histories

Program, 2005-2012 97/1/70, American Library Association Archives at the University of Illinois, Urbana-Champaign, 104:52.

26. George Cukor, et al., *The Philadelphia Story* (Burbank, CA: Warner Home Video, 2000 [released 1940]).

27. Walter Lang, et al., *Desk Set* (Beverly Hills, CA: Fox Video, 2004 [released 1957]).

28. J. Agada, "Studies of the Personality of Librarians," *Drexel Library Quarterly* 20(2), (1984), 24–45; B. I. Dewey, "Selection of Librarianship as a Career: Implications for Recruitment," *Journal of Education for Librarianship* 26(1), (1985), 16–24; K. M. Heim, *The Status of Women in Librarianship: Historical, Sociological, and Economic Issues* (New York: Neal-Schuman, 1983); R. Kneale, *You Don't Look Like a Librarian: Shattering Stereotypes and Creating Positive New Images in the Internet Age* (Medford, NJ: Information Today, 2009); L. C. Lancaster, "The Click and Clash of Generations," *Library Journal* 128(17), (2003), 36–39; K. Low, *Casanova Was a Librarian: A Light-Hearted Look at the Profession* (Jefferson, NC: McFarland, 2007); P. Wilson, *Stereotype and Status: Librarians in the United States* (Westport, CT: Greenwood Press, 1982).

29. Richwine, 87:45.

30. Rita Auerbach, interview by Kristy Raffensberger, June 11, 2008, audio recording, transcript, A. Arro Smith "Capturing Our Stories" Oral Histories Program, 2005-2012 97/1/70, American Library Association Archives at the University of Illinois, Urbana-Champaign, 02:58.

31. Ibid., 32:20.

32. Arlene Luster, interview by A. Arro Smith, July 11, 2009, video recording, transcript, A. Arro Smith "Capturing Our Stories" Oral Histories Program, 2005-2012 97/1/70, American Library Association Archives at the University of Illinois, Urbana-Champaign, 25:17.

33. Robert Gaines, interview by Anne Marie Taber, August 15, 2008, video recording, transcript, A. Arro Smith "Capturing Our Stories" Oral Histories Program, 2005-2012 97/1/70, American Library Association Archives at the University of Illinois, Urbana-Champaign, 06:35.

34. Yamashita, 40:53.

35. Ibid., 40:00.

36. Irene Hoadley, interview by Joan Heath and Arro Smith, April 27, 2010, video recording, transcript, A. Arro Smith "Capturing Our Stories" Oral Histories

Program, 2005-2012 97/1/70, American Library Association Archives at the University of Illinois, Urbana-Champaign, 31:34.

37. Breen, 24:12.

38. Patterson, 18:59.

39. Larson, 46:26.

40. Mary Bushing, interview by Kathy Kaya, June 6, 2010, video recording, transcript, A. Arro Smith "Capturing Our Stories" Oral Histories Program, 2005-2012 97/1/70, American Library Association Archives at the University of Illinois, Urbana-Champaign, 44:09.

41. Breen, 32:54.

Chapter 3

TECHNOLOGY MEMORIES

HOW TECHNOLOGICAL INNOVATION AFFECTED THE PROFESsional lives of our subjects is truly astonishing. This cohort of librarians ushered in much of the digital age that twenty-first-century librarians and library users take for granted. Their stories of the introduction of computers and automation are particularly fascinating. This chapter on technology memories has many subsections to account for the scope of these recollections. We will begin with precomputer technology and then discuss early computer technology, the introduction of online public access catalogs (OPACs), interlibrary loan (ILL), and online database searching. The chapter closes with librarians sharing regrets about how technology was implemented as well as some "lessons learned" about automation.

Precomputer Technology

Several librarians shared memories of precomputer technologies. "Library hand" was mentioned by both Sarah Long and Valerie Feinman. This handwriting style was a convention of cursive penmanship that was thought to be particularly legible and was used to create catalog card and index entries in the absence of a typewriter.

Ms. Feinman remembers hand copying citations that the reference librarians had collected to create a local history card index for the Hamilton, Ontario, public library in the 1940s and '50s. And thirty years later when she visited the library, that index with hundreds of cards in library hand—*her* library hand—was still being used because the Canadian News Index, which began publication in 1975, had never attempted any retrospective indexing.[1]

Sarah Long, past president of ALA, also recounts a library hand memory. Her library career—and her professional training—began after typewriters had become more commonplace, and she had never heard of library hand. But she was asked for a handwriting sample when interviewing for a position in England while her husband was studying there:

> **I applied for the job, and I went to the interview. And there was an older woman who interviewed me. And she asked me for a sample of my handwriting, and I thought, this—remember this is in the late '60s—I thought, "Cool, she's into handwriting analysis." Oh no no, she was interested in library hand. You know, where you write on the card catalog, the catalog cards and so on. Somehow, I think because I was sufficiently obscure to her, she gave me the job. And so I worked in a teacher training college in Bristol, England, for, I think, three years or so.**[2]

Creating a catalog and indexes were not the only processes that were manually performed—the entire library was an orchestrated, fully human endeavor. In addition to the card catalog in which each item was represented with a surrogate main entry card and then "traced" with additional entry cards for title(s), additional authors, and subject(s), a master file of shelflist cards was kept in the technical services department of the library. These were used to aid the cataloger in selecting the appropriate classification for new materials and to conduct an inventory of the collection.

Diana Collins remembers shelflist cards as "little three-by-five things of agony" when describing how an inventory was executed before catalog automation. The librarian would physically take a drawer of shelflist cards and go through the shelves item by item, matching materials with their surrogates. A missing book would then be checked within the circulation cards to see if it was charged to a patron. Ms. Collins worked at the Marble Falls, Texas, library, but the technical processing was done at the Burnet, Texas, library—so the shelflist resided thirteen miles away. Not only was her inventory a time-consuming task, it was also a coordination challenge.[3]

Early Computer Technology

The book catalog is another technology that many librarians remember prior to integrated library systems (ILSs). The *Encyclopedia of Library and Information Sciences* describes the book catalog as a technology that had existed in a primitive form for many years, but it became a practical tool after punch card computer technology made its compilation and revision less cumbersome, beginning around 1965 with the Baltimore County Public Library Book Catalog.[4] The book catalog enabled a library's complete catalog to be shared with multiple branches, partners, and researchers.

Pat Tuohy worked at the Austin, Texas, public library and shares her memories of the book catalog with an astonished—and much younger—librarian interviewer:

> **Pat Tuohy: Austin Public was considered kind of cutting edge technologically because they had a card catalog based on computer records. Now they developed a freestanding punch card system with the author, title, subject, and they created a book catalog—have you ever seen one?**

Jessica Kirkland: No, I haven't, I'm interested to see this.

PT: This is a book catalog.

JK: Lift it up, there we go. [Ms. Tuohy shows the videographer a large-format paperback book, *Subject Catalog A–F,* of approximately 1,200 pages.]

PT: And this is 1976 and I don't know when they started publishing this, but they went from the card catalog to the book catalog, and I'm not sure when they started doing this, maybe late '60s, early '70s, and there would be a punch card for each one of these titles and it was like this. And this is the subject, so you'd look up the subject, you'd look up the books, and you'd get a call number and as I recall, there were no locations, no locations, and there were at that time fifteen branches. . . . So you didn't know if you owned it, but you did know that it was owned by the system.[5]

Kent Middleton, also at the Austin Public Library, reports nearly identical memories of the technological advance that the book catalog brought to a system of several branches. He also has to explain what a book catalog is to his interviewer. He remembers that the final edition of the book catalog was printed in twelve very thick volumes.[6]

An interim catalog technology that existed between the book catalog and online automation was the microfilm or fiche catalog. It reduced the size of the mammoth book catalog to a few reels of microfilm or sheets of microfiche; however, it did require using a microform reader. None of the memories reported concerning the microform catalog were positive. Micki Freeny states, "That was horrible—that was really bad."[7] Kenneth Yamashita agrees:

We would have kids kind of spitting on the glass and then crunching the microfiche into the reader and, oh . . . it was terrible and

> **people not putting the fiche back in order and you know, uh . . . not good, not good at all.**[8]

The computers that existed to produce these book catalogs and microform catalogs in the 1960s, '70s, and '80s were by no means "personal computers." They were very large machines using punch cards to input data, and the data were stored on large reels of magnetic tape. *Desk Set,* the motion picture comedy released in 1957 and starring Katharine Hepburn as a corporate librarian, depicts the introduction of just such a machine.[9]

Many interviewees relate their early computer memories and how they could envision this technology as being a powerful force in their careers, but none claims to have ever correctly predicted the modern prevalence of the personal computer and its paradigm-changing impact on the profession.

Connie Corson and her husband, Richard, both librarians in New York City, volunteered to work at a pavilion during the 1964 World's Fair demonstrating an IBM punch card–based computer. As Ms. Corson is describing this memory, the interviewer specifically asks her about *Desk Set:*

> **Connie Corson: Librarians were asked if they would be willing to demonstrate information access. Well, this was the very beginning, you know, of the introduction of computers and both Richard, my husband, and I, we took a two-week training course with IBM and then we were in an IBM pavilion at the, you know, at the fair. . . . But right behind, you know, they had a whole bay of tables where we were sitting and people could come in and ask us information questions and, you know, we had to use punch cards to get at the information.**
>
> **Jane Fitzpatrick: Wow. That's something.**

CC: So that was, I mean, an unusual experience.

JF: Absolutely.

CC: And, you know, something that kind of made me—gave me a sense of what might come. And this huge, I mean, I would say the mainframe computer was probably as large as one of the walls here, you know, humming behind us.

JF: Did it make you feel like Spencer Tracy and Katharine Hepburn in that movie [laughter] where he pits her against the machine but she wins—the librarian?

CC: Well, no, that didn't quite happen [laughter].[10]

Kenneth Yamashita spent some of his professional career as an early library automation vendor representative. When discussing how he would attempt to convince librarians to adopt the automated LIS paradigm, he inadvertently harkens back to one of the plot elements of *Desk Set.* The women in the motion picture are initially convinced that the "electronic brain" is being deployed so their positions can be eliminated. The computer engineer insists the machine is being installed to "create more leisure" for the librarians.[11] The librarians interpret "more leisure" as a signal that they will soon be unemployed. Dr. Yamashita states:

The way we were trained to sell these systems was I think—I think at that time it was—it was so that it would—displace some of the more routine mundane tasks for the staff so that they could concentrate on public services or that you would not need to have as many staff.[12]

At the conclusion of *Desk Set*, the librarians are told by the computer engineer (played by Spencer Tracy) that their jobs were never in jeopardy. The machine was "never intended to take over. It was never intended to replace you. It's here to free your time for research. It's here to help you."[13]

OPACs

Rita Auerbach remembers visiting Stanford University, which had an online catalog that shared resources with UC Berkeley and one other university. She remembers thinking how that technology would eliminate the time-consuming filing of catalog cards. This same memory regarding the drudgery of filing catalog cards is also reported by Gail Hueting: "Nobody was gladder than me when OPACs came in and we didn't have to do filing anymore." She remembers there never being a time in her career before the online catalog when there was not a backlog of cards to be filed.[14]

Dr. Dale Ricklefs remembers hating not the filing of the catalog cards but the manual typing and proofing of multiple cards. Before she had a computer that could create cards, she would create a stencil and produce a master card using a mimeograph machine, then edit each card's heading. She admits that the "cards looked like '*bleep*,' but [laughter], but it didn't matter—it was there and I didn't have to proof them all."[15] She acquired her first computer to print better-looking cards using a program for the Apple IIe in 1983.

For cataloger Sandy Berman, automation of the catalog meant that subject headings could be reconsidered—and easily changed—as knowledge expanded and ideas about history and culture were refined. Changing a heading no longer meant physically extracting the cards, remanufacturing them, and then refiling them. A subject could be changed with a universal Find and Replace database command. This capability liberated catalogers to devise more ethical subject headings:

> **That was the new thing, but that automated database also meant that . . . you could, like, do some changing without having to change—like, changing a heading, the form of it or adding a cross-reference or whatever—without having to go run to the card catalog and alter a catalog card every time, or dozens of them or hundreds of them. So you could change from Mohammadism to Islam relatively simply. Sometimes you also had to change subdivision forms, but you didn't have to change every damn card that had been Mohammadism to Islam. That would be like a global, they say global change or something near it. . . .**
>
> **And then we would change things. . . . For instance, if we had a heading for Kafirs, we changed that to either, you know, Blacks . . . or Zulu. . . . Anyway, it was just easier to do it in an automated mode so I think the bosses realized what we could do and I was certainly willing once in this milieu to use what was available to us. Now, I was about to say something ironic. Well, the ironic thing is that we were really doing this thanks to real work, you know, computer work that had been done at New York Public Library, which produced their own book catalogs. The irony is that within a year or two we were using their automated systems in ways that they weren't. Like we would change, did change from Near East to Middle East which I don't think is a contentious matter. It is just that all the literature and language was going Middle East. It wasn't Near East anymore.[16]**

Online catalogs and library circulation automation were not universally embraced. Robert Gaines distinctly remembers that there were faculty members bitterly opposed to replacing the card catalog. He was a librarian at the University of North Carolina at Greensboro and was sent on a fact-finding mission to the UNC campus at Charlotte, to Virginia Tech, and to the University of Kentucky, among other institutions that had already automated.

> **And when we finally did get the system up—and I'm thinking this was 1984—we thought this was successful and well done. It's nothing like the web-based systems, you know, that we have today, but it gave you many, many more access points than an old card catalog. It still took us quite a while to convince the teaching faculty that this was going to be much better for them and their students—and it took many one-on-one demonstrations to drive that point home. But after a while, most of them came around, but if they didn't come around, they retired.[17]**

Micki Freeny also remembers that the transition to an integrated library system was difficult for many librarians, technical services staff, and circulation clerks. She states that many older employees simply chose to retire instead of learning the new skills required. But both Ms. Freeny and Richard Corson recall being excited by the technological change, despite the pain of the transition. Mr. Corson says that at the beginning of his career in 1962, the most advanced technology they possessed was a manual typewriter. He describes the arc of his career as beginning with nineteenth-century technology and jumping to the twenty-first century. This is one of the reasons he enjoyed his work so much.

Many librarians remember their first personal computer, or minicomputer—as opposed to the early mainframes described earlier. Dr. Ricklefs remembers her excitement when her library acquired its first IBM 8086, because it had a hard drive: "It had a hard drive. Woo-hoo! A hard drive."[18] Dr. Bill Mears had access to a Radio Shack computer at his library at Southwest Texas State University. When one of his associates suggested that the library purchase a newer computer with a 4K memory, he remembers saying, "Four K, what are they going to do with all that? [Laughter]"[19]

But for many librarians, the real power of computing was in the ability to share and retrieve resources remotely. There are two strains of these memories: the advance in interlibrary loan processing, and the periodical databases that became available.

OCLC

Andrew Hansen talks of precomputerized interlibrary loan (ILL) as a virtual black hole that research librarians flailed in without precision or great success. At the beginning of his career, ILL was a possibility, but the request had to be accompanied with a written justification for its necessity to the researcher. And each request was sent to the nearest large library, simply hoping it would own the item and might be willing to loan it.[20]

Irene Hoadley worked at Ohio State University in the mid-1960s when her boss, Dr. Lewis Branscomb, directed her and a team of others to formulate a proposal for university libraries to share a computerized union list of materials that would facilitate an automated interlibrary loan system. This modest proposal was then presented to Fred Kilgour and then it became what we know as OCLC (formerly the Ohio College Library Center, now known as the Online Computer Library Center). When the interviewer asks Dr. Hoadley if she could even imagine how her "Inter-university Council" proposal would ultimately shape the future of librarianship, she simply responds, "No."[21]

Ironically, Dr. Hoadley insisted on never having a computer in her own office. When she retired as the director of the Texas A&M University library in 1992, personal computers were becoming more pervasive, but as a director she could still delegate computer-related duties to her assistants.

OCLC also revolutionized cataloging. Gail Hueting, Richard Corson, and Billie Grace Herring all mention how OCLC made cataloging so much more efficient. Janet Swan Hill, a cataloger at Northwestern University, notes that computer-generated copy-cataloging was possible prior to OCLC, but it involved purchasing tapes from the Library of Congress, mounting the tapes to the library's mainframe, and searching locally. OCLC made a union list of MARC records that was updated daily available for import. In addition to providing a platform for interlibrary loan, it made cataloging materials an efficient, shared responsibility.

When I asked Ms. Hill about ethical issues in her career, she was quick to point out that library ethics extend past censorship and public services. "Authority control is an ethical issue. Do you go ahead and do the work to save others the work? Cooperative cataloging is an ethical issue. Do you sponge or do you contribute?"[22] She also noted that training new librarians and working with interns are ethical decisions to contribute to the legacy of the profession.

Online Database Searching

The advent of online databases truly brought the world of research to any library with a telephone connection, a personal computer with a modem, and the financial resources to afford a pricey subscription invoiced by the second, plus applicable long-distance charges.

Because of the cost involved, early database searches were anything but spontaneous. A researcher would submit a request to a librarian who would formulate an efficient search string using Boolean operators. Once the local machine was connected to a database via telephone modem, this search string would have to be typed in very carefully using a DOS-based interface. One false keystroke could deliver line after line of incorrect results—while the clock continued to advance and the invoice continued to grow. Jennifer John Patterson recalls her first database search with horror: Her boss had requested some research on calcium so Ms. Patterson typed in *calcium* with no additional Boolean operators. The machine printed out a stack of dot-matrix pages that were more or less useless—and very expensive.[23]

Medical libraries were generally the first to take advantage of database searching. Sheila Henderson remembers using a National Library of Medicine database as early as 1972. Valerie Feinman recalls using a predecessor of MEDLINE, called MEDLARS, as early as the late 1960s. She remembers this as an exciting time in her career, attending a three-day training session with other medical librarians. She has a particularly entertaining story from this time:

> **We were in Syracuse until '69. So I did a whole lot of different projects at the Medical Center that were absolutely fun and way ahead of anything else. So, I guess one of the funniest things there was after I showed a faculty—a professor—how to use MEDLARS, and was searching on an operation that he was going to do in a couple of days, we actually found him a brand new article. And the next morning at nine o'clock, I got a phone call. He was in the operating room—would I please bring the article to him because he had forgotten one section of it. And we got it back at the end of the day with a little bit of blood on it. [We] wiped it off and put it back on the shelf.**
>
> **I mean, that—every medical librarian has a story like that—similar to this, but I lived this as a librarian in the '60s, who was very, very young and raw, actually. [Laughs] So, it was fun.**[24]

The cost of the database searching—and whether to pass that cost directly to the researcher—was an ethical dilemma the new technology introduced. Nancy Fogarty discusses this concern when remembering the early days of database searching. This issue plagued the administration of her library at the University of North Carolina because charging a fee for research work was a paradigm change. The student or faculty member would sign a contract submitted with his database research request stipulating the maximum charge he would allow: $25, $30, sometimes up to $50. "It was a very controversial thing, charging for information."[25]

Librarians began letting researchers conduct their own database searches as the price of telecommunications dropped and more user-friendly search interfaces were developed. Peggy Richwine remembers the shift beginning to occur in 1987. Before that year she would spend a great deal of energy conducting database searches on behalf of researchers at her academic library. But then her duties shifted from being an information intermediary to being a trainer. Technology allowed library patrons to become more independent, even for advanced research; reference librarians became technology tutors and counselors, facilitating the enterprise.

Valerie Feinman relates another humorous story about teaching students how to shift from database to database within a single interface: "One of the instructions was to press F9 to transfer to a different database. The students had to have it explained that this meant not to touch *F* and then *9*."[26] However, another librarian, Connie Corson, a school librarian in New York City, ultimately found that her best technical support for her early EBSCO database terminal came from her young students. When she found herself befuddled while attempting to sort out all the cords and connections, she remembers one of them patting her back and saying, "Don't worry, Mrs. Corson, we'll be there for you. We'll help you."[27]

Some Lessons Learned Regarding New Technologies

Several librarians brought up some collection development dangers that database technology introduced. Dale Ricklefs, Valerie Feinman, and Kent Middleton all shared similar concerns about administrative shortsightedness in the zeal to embrace online databases.

Dr. Ricklefs was pained by the fact that many libraries are now wholly dependent on database subscriptions. Where they used to have stacks of periodical back issues—or cabinets of microfilm—they now possess nothing tangible but contracts that might not be renewed during a budget shortfall. Some current subscriptions might have been eliminated during previous budget crises at a library, but the collection of past (hard-copy) serials was still intact for researchers and patrons to access. Now entire serials collections are dependent on the whim of budgetary authorities and digital vendors. Without hard copies of past issues, the entire serials department may vanish if a subscription is not renewed.

Kent Middleton expressed the same disenchantment. As the head of reference services at the central Austin Public Library, he was initially very excited about the promise of this technology. But through the course of his career, he saw the standing-order print subscriptions budget drawn down to purchase the database subscriptions. And then the database budget was drawn down because of budget issues—but the print subscriptions budget was never adjusted up. He also laments the fact that his institution—and the profession as a whole—has not successfully educated the public about the database resources. Researchers know how to access the articles using library databases, but the average patron who would come into the library in the past and enjoy the plethora of hard-copy magazines in the reading room are simply left out of the new digital calculus.

Valerie Feinman remembers a premature leap into technology—although it was microform technology. Her library had decades of *Godey's Lady's Book*, *The Century*, and other serials that had been popular at the end of the nineteenth century and were taking up many linear feet of shelving. A decision was made to embrace the new technology and replace the back files with microfiche copies. But the great illustrations and advertisements did not make a successful transition to black-and-white microform:

> **When I saw the microfilm, I cried because it didn't have all the ads and all the pictures. And the ads are what students loved, because in a marketing and business course, they wanted to look at an ad from the 1880s and compare it to one from the 1930s compared to one from the 1980s.**[28]

She was very happy to see a retrospective digital version—in color—of *Godey's Lady's Book* at a vendor's booth during the 2008 ALA Annual Conference; she felt that technology was finally redeeming that particular format transition mistake from her early career.

Technology Regrets

Ms. Feinman's regret concerning the deaccessioning of *Godey's Lady's Book* is but one voice of disenchantment that the promise of digital technologies brought to the profession of librarianship. The fact is that the World Wide Web and broadband connectivity radically changed how libraries operated and how librarians did their jobs. Though no one wished that digital technologies had not penetrated their profession, many shared wistful memories of library work before the digital age.

Filomena Magavero, who began her career in 1946, remembers how she often felt like a detective when doing research. She worked at a maritime college library, and its collection included materials on seamanship dating back to the nineteenth century. As she became more and more acquainted with the collection, her personal memory became more valuable than any finding aid or index. She developed personal relationships with the researchers in her field because of her expertise. She reports:

> **I used to love digging into those things, you know, trying to find an elusive fact that they wanted to know about a particular vessel, and we could do it because we had the resources. And after awhile, you know, people knew that. And it was fun to get a phone call asking for me by name, you know, because I had done something for somebody else, you know? But it was really great fun. I was sorry when the computers came in [laughs].**[29]

Mary Bushing talks about technology taking the humanity out of the craft of librarianship. When she visits her community library in Bozeman, Montana, she rarely interacts with any of the staff. The catalog is user-friendly and allows her to put materials on hold if it shows them to be checked out, and the circulation desk is fully self-service with an automated scanner for self-checkout. She is quick to point out that the building is beautiful—an award-winning, LEED-certified building—and the atmosphere is pleasant, but she misses interacting with librarians and clerks. "As we create some of these efficiencies—which I am all for—we have to understand that relationships matter."[30]

Andrew Hansen, a public librarian, remembers his pre-Internet reference department attempting to answer a question about Danish Constitution Day. Three different librarians were trying to determine when the Danish Constitution had been signed. And they all came back with three different answers. It turned out that the Danish Constitution is never amended: when a revision is necessary, a whole new document is created. Three different dates had been found in three different reference books, depending on the age of the reference. The librarian's job in this case was not just finding the answer or answers but figuring out why there were different answers.

Mr. Hansen has not re-created this reference query in the digital age, but he posits that Google would be just as accurate—perhaps delivering even more than three "correct" answers. He sees the role of the modern librarian as one of an information consultant: someone who can cipher the right answer out of the calculus of Google.

Many librarians expressed regret about digital technology while quickly following up with celebrations of the online world. Karlan Sick laments that young people cannot understand a lecture today unless it is accompanied by a PowerPoint presentation, but then just as quickly rejoices that digital media seem to have sparked a renaissance in young people's reading and literature—and curiosity.

Bill Mears began witnessing the changing role of reference librarianship when he was the director of the Southwest Texas State University library in the 1990s. Even though he was the library director, he always scheduled a couple of shifts at the reference desk each week—to keep his finger on the pulse of the library and to relieve the tedium of administrative work. After he retired from the university, he took what was supposed to be a very short-term position as interim director at a small public library in central Texas. At that library he was the only professional staff member for much of his tenure—and he spent a great deal of time at the reference desk. He could quite clearly see how online technology had changed the role of the reference librarian, yet he was unsure of what that role actually was. He reports that whenever he would bring up this topic—of a changing role for libraries and librarians—at professional conferences and meetings, his colleagues would vehemently disagree with him. He remembers one meeting where he was pulled aside by a colleague and told that he was totally wrong.

Rita Auerbach misses the days when there was no Internet and the quest for information began and ended at the library, when "they didn't labor under the misconception that the Internet was as good as a trained librarian."[31]

In pre-digital days, the library (card) catalog and resources (books) were completely under the control of library staff. There were never surprises unless hooligan children rearranged the drawers of the card catalog. Nancy Clark Fogarty points out the unanticipated consequences of technology, especially from third-party vendors. Overnight and without any warning, a database interface could change radically, or the OPAC vendor could change how records were indexed—and entire fields of information would vanish without notice. Technology may have freed up her time to devote to other tasks, but monitoring and troubleshooting the technology proved to be very time consuming. She, too, is quick to point out that the efficiency of the modern "connected" library is worth all the trouble, but learning to spot the trouble involved a significant learning curve.

Jennifer John Patterson misses her early days as a business librarian using "paper" resources. She fondly remembers how the reference department had a little competition to see who could answer a telephone reference question while the patron was still on the phone—instead of noting the question and calling the patron back later with the answer.

Using the paper—or analog—reference sources, which were the only things available when she began her career, took expertise and personal memory that the average person did not possess. This is what separated librarians from lay researchers: a strong background in information resources, the tools to quickly extract the desired information, and an often encyclopedic memory.

Ms. Patterson often thought of herself as a "magic helper":

> **Well, when I was in library school, I took a course with Glynn Harmon and it was an information science course. And at the end of my time in library school, we had a written exam and an oral interview. That was as much as we did to complete our master's degree. And on the written exam, one of the essay questions was, "Compare the term 'magic helper' with the term 'information scientist.'" And I defended the concept of "magic helper." And they wouldn't graduate me unless I rewrote that part of the essay and said, "No, I can see why it's important to be an information scientist."**
>
> **But really to me, that was the essence of librarianship—that was what drew me to it—was that ability to magically connect someone with what they needed the most to know. And it was like magic. It was like something that you could do for people that they could not easily do for themselves.**
>
> **And as we moved into the current era, it is much much more obvious because of Google—because of search engines—how to find what you need to know, and so that role has indeed pretty much gone away. The only thing that is still left of it to me is readers' advisory. That is still very personal and very magical when you can find the books that someone really wants to read that they don't even know exist. So that is there, but it has indeed progressed to a much more self-service approach to information seeking. And that was happening all during my career.**[32]

The provision of web access in libraries quickly brought a very controversial challenge to librarians: whether to filter. And the early filters were not particularly effective. Some libraries elected to filter everything, some decided to implement a tiered policy, and others made the decision—backed by ALA policies on censorship—to not restrict Internet access.[33]

Micki Freeny reports that several members of her staff left because of the challenge of providing Internet service. "I think there were lots of people who said, 'I'm not going to learn to use a computer, and I don't need to be here for that.'"[34] She remembers that many librarians found monitoring patrons' use of the computers to be beyond the scope of what they had envisioned for their professional lives. Reference librarians found themselves performing far fewer reference transactions. Instead of doing the work they loved, they were reduced to scheduling Internet time on a clipboard for patrons who were often uncooperative—and policing Internet users for inappropriate content viewing.

Technology did eventually catch up to the modern librarian's needs. Time- and print-management software was developed and successfully implemented in the new wired library. Ms. Freeny concludes this section of her interview with a story of how technology even redeemed itself for the traditional reference librarian:

> **One of the biggest changes was the use of [the] telephone. Because at our bigger branches, and especially the one where I was the manager for a long time, the telephone business was phenomenal. . . . That telephone reference just went by the wayside. And they saw that—and this was what was frustrating for the frontline staff—that was replaced in their workday with monitoring computers. So that was very frustrating.**
>
> **I found a lot of good reference librarians revitalized when we went to live online chat reference. It gave them that old-fashioned reference experience that they all enjoyed. So I think that was, in a way, a savior for the staff that was nostalgic for the kind of reference work they used to do.**[35]

Sarah Long was the 1999–2000 ALA president during the height of the Internet filtering controversy. ALA took a strong anti-filtering stand based on concepts from the *Intellectual Freedom Manual*.[36] Ms. Long was the public face of ALA defending libraries from the threat of government-mandated censorship, such as legislation that became known as CIPA (Child Internet Protection Act). The brave new world of the Internet meant that Ms. Long was barraged by the press and pundits accusing her of advocating for the availability of pornography in public libraries—clearly a misconstrued notion of the ALA policy on filtering. "Dr. Laura" Schlessinger led a months-long campaign against public libraries concerning this issue on a widely distributed syndicated radio talk show.[37]

But it was not just the media that did not understand the full dimensions of the issue: Ms. Long's own family confronted her with accusations. She recalls an uncomfortable conversation in her own kitchen with her stepson, holding his infant son, when he asked Ms. Long if she really wanted the baby to be exposed to smut at the library. "I certainly approved of ALA's position, but it is very hard to be the point person. And to be pummeled with those kinds of questions—."[38]

Technology Redemption

Dr. Mears is not the only retiring librarian expressing ideas about the changing role of the library. Several other interviewees tempered their technology memories with advice for the next generation of librarians regarding the future role of the library in an online age.

Kent Middleton echoes Rita Auerbach's sentiment about the mistaken notion that the Internet is as good as a trained librarian. He discusses the lost opportunity to educate people about the Internet. Mr. Middleton sees the library's new role as instructing patrons how to find authoritative information, although he worries that the time for that may be too late—everyone already thinks they are Internet experts. Kathy Kaya expresses the same sentiment. She sees students who have already learned inefficient—lazy—research habits:

> **The students are so savvy that they have created—before they get to us, they have created their own way of looking for information without the—without the background of being able to judge whether it is good information, whether it's appropriate for their purpose. And so I—and this was true when I was working, but I suspect that it's maybe even greater—that it's having to undo bad habits rather than just teaching them anew.**[39]

She does believe that technology has made it easier for librarians to "concentrate on librariness and not having to worry about the details and the nitty-gritty of making things work,"[40] but that new "librariness" must be about teaching people how to evaluate the information they find for themselves.

Janet Swan Hill and I discussed how the cataloger's craft is even more important in a digital age. Cataloging used to be about creating surrogate records (catalog cards) so humans could locate actual physical materials (books). Though library cataloging led the information age and the content of these surrogates is now called "metadata," catalogers are still doing the same essential task: creating efficient tools for finding information.

We both lamented the lack of attention that is focused on cataloging in the digital age. Because most of the population now believes they can find anything and everything they desire using Google, even some library administrators see the cataloger's work as redundant. What very few non-catalogers realize is that the web is completely dependent on metadata—and the creation of metadata is what catalogers do. In this digital millennium, the cataloger's work is even more important because so much of research depends on searching through the surrogate records we create, and finding materials serendipitously in the stacks of a library is a luxury few can afford.

Peggy Richwine voices a similar concern about having a standard vocabulary of subject headings. If an article does not possess metadata from a standard thesaurus of subject headings, a researcher may very well miss many valuable sources. Ms. Richwine gives the example of an article about a newborn. Some writers will call this person an infant; others will refer to this person as a neonate. It is the judicious application of standardized metadata—what catalogers have always done—that makes research efficient.

Ms. Hill laments many trends in the technical services departments of today's libraries and the fact that cataloging education is waning in the country's LIS programs. She is worried that library administrators are decreasing the funding for technical services because of the mistaken impression that online resources can be efficiently located through a keyword search. "We don't have a profession if we don't have information organization. There is no point in our existing as a separate discipline without it."[41] In a world totally dependent on digital information, "the metadata is even more important than it used to be."[42] Dorothy McGarry echoes Ms. Hill's worries about LIS education: "I think libraries are getting shortchanged by turning out people who can call themselves librarians who haven't had a decent class in cataloging. Or any class in cataloging."[43]

Anne Gault describes the vicissitudes of technology as a "merry-go-round that you have to grab and get in there."[44] She still prefers to read a book and does not see that changing.

Sheila Ross Henderson is excited about the modern library. She believes that providing Internet stations for the public encouraged more men to visit her library than she had seen in her entire career before the advent of the computer. Ms. Henderson always had a contingent of retired men who would come to read the paper or check their portfolios using Morningstar, but working and professional men began to be patrons when she added computers, online databases, and Internet access:

> **Now I have businessmen there. There are accountants. I have one doctor that comes on a regular basis. I have the manager—well, he is actually the owner—of the McDonald's that comes and does his accounting, and, you know, his books and all that in the library.**
>
> **We have become a community hub for all walks of life and I think that is just magnificent. They love our wireless. I had a policeman tell me, "I ran somebody off from your library the other night." I said, "What happened?" "Well, he was out there using your wireless." I said, "Don't do that." [Laughter] I said, "You are supposed to put that down," I said, "so I can count it on my statistics." He looked at me, but that's—I mean, we want people to use our services and if having wireless that is accessible outside the door is going to help somebody, I'm all for it.[45]**

Nancy Fogarty has many interesting memories about how technology affected academic librarianship over the course of her career, but when asked about the most important skill she learned in preparation for a career in librarianship, she cites the ability to have good interpersonal relations and the ability to type fast. At the end of her interview—after discussing the myriad ways technology became incorporated with "old-fashioned library science"—her advice to new librarians is to "master the content and the format." And the skill that has been the most useful? "Typing."[46]

Jeannette Larson states that the days when the librarian was in direct control of the library collection are over. She recalls when the librarians of smaller libraries would be expected to know about every book in the collection—that was their job. She feels the biggest challenge for modern librarians is an adjustment to a new paradigm of the collection: a collection that is constantly evolving and in flux. Ms. Larson believes the librarian's new job is similar to "readers' advisory," but for the information age: knowing how to direct patrons to the information and materials they need, on their level of understanding. It is about learning to manage information and facilitating its efficient dissemination among the library's constituents.

Sarah Long refers to her previous comments about precomputer technology to discuss—provoke—ways that libraries will need to evolve to meet the needs of future users:

> **Remember I talked about library hand? This is when cards were written for the card catalog with a certain—with a certain penmanship. I mean, that's laughable now. And young librarians graduating today don't even know what that means. And so, now I think, for example, we ought to think about a library not cataloging anything in the traditional way at all. You know, I think maybe Dewey might be on the way out. We have tagging now.**
>
> **This is kinda—I'm speaking heresy here. And I'm speaking to be provocative, but I think librarianship has to think about those people born after 19—9, what am I saying—after 1980, because those people are very different from you and me. They have grown up with games, gaming. They are into multitasking. They do things very differently, and there is some evidence they even think differently. And the library has to be a very different place for them.**[47]

NOTES

1. Valerie Feinman, interview by Sarah Albert, June 29, 2008, video recording, transcript, A. Arro Smith "Capturing Our Stories" Oral Histories Program, 2005-2012 97/1/70, American Library Association Archives at the University of Illinois, Urbana-Champaign, 09:30.
2. Sarah Ann Long, interview by Ninfa Trejo, June 27, 2008, video recording, transcript, A. Arro Smith "Capturing Our Stories" Oral Histories Program, 2005-2012 97/1/70, American Library Association Archives at the University of Illinois, Urbana-Champaign, 05:15.
3. Diana Collins, interview by Jessica Kirkland, November 16, 2008, video recording, transcript, A. Arro Smith "Capturing Our Stories" Oral Histories

Program, 2005-2012 97/1/70, American Library Association Archives at the University of Illinois, Urbana-Champaign, 19:25.

4. Jay E. Daily and Eugene R. Hanson, "Catalogs and Cataloging: History," *Encyclopedia of Library and Information Sciences*, 3rd ed. (New York: Taylor and Francis, 2009), 818–54.
5. Patricia Tuohy, interview by Jessica Kirkland, June 17, 2009, video recording, transcript, A. Arro Smith "Capturing Our Stories" Oral Histories Program, 2005-2012 97/1/70, American Library Association Archives at the University of Illinois, Urbana-Champaign, 24:18.
6. Kent Middleton, interview by Gustavo Soto, November 12, 2008, video recording, transcript, A. Arro Smith "Capturing Our Stories" Oral Histories Program, 2005-2012 97/1/70, American Library Association Archives at the University of Illinois, Urbana-Champaign, 14:10.
7. Micki Freeny, interview by A. Arro Smith, July 10, 2009, video recording, transcript, A. Arro Smith "Capturing Our Stories" Oral Histories Program, 2005-2012 97/1/70, American Library Association Archives at the University of Illinois, Urbana-Champaign, 28:55.
8. Kenneth Yamashita, interview by A. Arro Smith, June 28, 2010, video recording, transcript, A. Arro Smith "Capturing Our Stories" Oral Histories Program, 2005-2012 97/1/70, American Library Association Archives at the University of Illinois, Urbana-Champaign, 35:48.
9. Walter Lang, et al., *Desk Set* (Beverly Hills, CA: Fox Video, 2004 [released 1957]).
10. Connie (Cornelia) Corson, interview by Jane Brodsky Fitzpatrick, August 3, 2009, audio recording, transcript, A. Arro Smith "Capturing Our Stories" Oral Histories Program, 2005-2012 97/1/70, American Library Association Archives at the University of Illinois, Urbana-Champaign, 53:51.
11. Lang.
12. Yamashita, 20:34.
13. Lang.
14. Gail Hueting, interview by Kathryn La Barre, April 29, 2011, video recording, transcript, A. Arro Smith "Capturing Our Stories" Oral Histories Program, 2005-2012 97/1/70, American Library Association Archives at the University of Illinois, Urbana-Champaign, 06:00.

15. Dale Ricklefs, interview by A. Arro Smith, Stephanie Langenkamp, and Pat Tuohy, April 8, 2011, video recording, transcript, A. Arro Smith "Capturing Our Stories" Oral Histories Program, 2005-2012 97/1/70, American Library Association Archives at the University of Illinois, Urbana-Champaign, 53:35.
16. Sandy (Sanford) Berman, interview by Tina Gross, August 18, 2012, video recording, transcript, A. Arro Smith "Capturing Our Stories" Oral Histories Program, 2005-2012 97/1/70, American Library Association Archives at the University of Illinois, Urbana-Champaign, 93:32.
17. Robert Gaines, interview by Anne Marie Taber, August 15, 2008, video recording, transcript, A. Arro Smith "Capturing Our Stories" Oral Histories Program, 2005-2012 97/1/70, American Library Association Archives at the University of Illinois, Urbana-Champaign, 27:44.
18. Ricklefs, 53:35.
19. Bill Mears, interview by Stephanie Langenkamp and Arro Smith, February 29, 2007, video recording, transcript, A. Arro Smith "Capturing Our Stories" Oral Histories Program, 2005-2012 97/1/70, American Library Association Archives at the University of Illinois, Urbana-Champaign, 23:06.
20. Andrew Hansen, interview by A. Arro Smith, July 13, 2009, video recording, transcript, A. Arro Smith "Capturing Our Stories" Oral Histories Program, 2005-2012 97/1/70, American Library Association Archives at the University of Illinois, Urbana-Champaign, 18:50.
21. Irene Hoadley, interview by Joan Heath and Arro Smith, April 27, 2010, video recording, transcript, A. Arro Smith "Capturing Our Stories" Oral Histories Program, 2005-2012 97/1/70, American Library Association Archives at the University of Illinois, Urbana-Champaign, 24:58.
22. Janet Swan Hill, interview by A. Arro Smith, June 26, 2010, video recording, transcript, A. Arro Smith "Capturing Our Stories" Oral Histories Program, 2005-2012 97/1/70, American Library Association Archives at the University of Illinois, Urbana-Champaign, 48:30.
23. Jennifer John Patterson, interview by Jennifer Jones, November 12, 2008, video recording, transcript, A. Arro Smith "Capturing Our Stories" Oral Histories Program, 2005-2012 97/1/70, American Library Association Archives at the University of Illinois, Urbana-Champaign, 18:58.
24. Feinman, 19:45.

25. Nancy Clark Fogarty, interview by Anne Marie Taber, August 20, 2008, video recording, transcript, A. Arro Smith "Capturing Our Stories" Oral Histories Program, 2005-2012 97/1/70, American Library Association Archives at the University of Illinois, Urbana-Champaign, 30:36.
26. Feinman, 01:25.
27. C. Corson, 41:07.
28. Feinman, 28:00.
29. Filomena Magavero, interview by Jane Brodsky Fitzpatrick, November 3, 2005, audio recording, transcript, A. Arro Smith "Capturing Our Stories" Oral Histories Program, 2005-2012 97/1/70, American Library Association Archives at the University of Illinois, Urbana-Champaign, 25:09.
30. Mary Bushing, interview by Kathy Kaya, June 6, 2010, video recording, transcript, A. Arro Smith "Capturing Our Stories" Oral Histories Program, 2005-2012 97/1/70, American Library Association Archives at the University of Illinois, Urbana-Champaign, 27:06.
31. Rita Auerbach, interview by Kristy Raffensberger, June 11, 2008, audio recording, transcript, A. Arro Smith "Capturing Our Stories" Oral Histories Program, 2005-2012 97/1/70, American Library Association Archives at the University of Illinois, Urbana-Champaign, 35:01.
32. Patterson, 28:49.
33. A. Arro Smith, "Internet Filtering Policy and Attitudes in Texas Public Libraries," *Texas Library Journal* 82(4), (2006), 148–51.
34. Freeny, 32:17.
35. Ibid.
36. American Library Association, Office for Intellectual Freedom, *Intellectual Freedom Manual,* 8th ed. (Chicago: American Library Association, 2010).
37. M. Wessells, "I Faced Dr. Laura—and Survived!," *American Libraries* 31(10), (2000), 56.
38. Long, 28:56.
39. Kathy Kaya, interview by Mary Bushing, June 6, 2010, video recording, transcript, A. Arro Smith "Capturing Our Stories" Oral Histories Program, 2005-2012 97/1/70, American Library Association Archives at the University of Illinois, Urbana-Champaign, 18:54.

40. Ibid., 20:31.

41. Hill, 43:38.

42. Ibid., 19:51.

43. Dorothy McGarry, interview by John Myers and Arro Smith, January 15, 2010, video recording, transcript, A. Arro Smith "Capturing Our Stories" Oral Histories Program, 2005-2012 97/1/70, American Library Association Archives at the University of Illinois, Urbana-Champaign, 59:29.

44. Anne Gault, interview by Jessica Kirkland, June 17, 2009, video recording, transcript, A. Arro Smith "Capturing Our Stories" Oral Histories Program, 2005-2012 97/1/70, American Library Association Archives at the University of Illinois, Urbana-Champaign, 12:14.

45. Sheila Ross Henderson, interview by Cathy Prazak, April 15, 2010, video recording, transcript, A. Arro Smith "Capturing Our Stories" Oral Histories Program, 2005-2012 97/1/70, American Library Association Archives at the University of Illinois, Urbana-Champaign, 22:57.

46. Fogarty, 58:35.

47. Long, 21:30.

Chapter 4

REGRETS

IN THIS CHAPTER WE LOOK AT REGRETS THAT LIBRARIANS voiced about their careers. Librarian salaries are so low compared to vocations that require even less education that it is almost a cliché. But our interviewees take the low pay in stride because they love their jobs. Another regret that many expressed—and that may very well be tied to the low wages librarians receive—is that of sexism. Librarianship has traditionally been a women's vocation, and some regret that fact.

The most salient—and surprising—regret identified by the retirees is very counterintuitive. Over and over in the interviews, end-of-career librarians express regret for leaving the work they originally became librarians to do—work with patrons—for the more prestigious work of administering a large organization or institution. We will start with regrets about successful promotion.

Promotion Regrets

Regret associated with moving up the administrative ladder is a pervasive theme within the corpus of interviews. It is a bittersweet regret because the promotion to higher levels of administration comes with increased pay and prestige, but almost all the respondents expressed regret about leaving behind the simplicity—and fun—of their former entry-level library duties.

In an academic library this regret might manifest itself as the added strain of faculty or tenure status and its attendant pressures. Kathryn Kaya refers to this as "jumping through hoops" when she would have been perfectly happy just working with students and helping the teaching faculty—"doing library things."[1] She made a conscious decision to not advance higher into administration because "it would have taken me too far from the work that I enjoyed doing—which was with the patrons."[2]

Other librarians, like Bill Mears, loved their work as administrators. Dr. Mears's master's degree was in librarianship, but his doctorate was in public administration. Though he was the director of a large academic library, his interviewer—a former employee—asked him about his habit of continuing to take reference shifts, even as the director. Dr. Mears responds to her question with the following, in a charming and self-effacing style:

> **I could say a lot of noble reasons—but it was because I liked working with the public. That's the bottom line of it. I truly found that much more enjoyable than pushing paper all day long. And so it was almost a relief to get out and work with the public. But I really liked working with the public. I like to do reference, because it's kind of like solving a puzzle—you know—finding the right answer. And because people usually appreciate that—and appreciate you—is another rewarding part of it.**[3]

This sentiment is echoed by Andrew Hansen, who began his career as a public librarian and then worked for many years as an administrator for the American Library Association. After he retired, he hoped to find a volunteer or part-time job as a traditional reference librarian, "doing what I really love doing. I did not want any part of administration."[4]

One public librarian, Sheila Henderson, also expresses resentment about the time that administration took away from what she saw as the library's mission, especially concerning personnel issues. Although she was adamant about the importance of coaching and mentoring early-career librarians, she also believed in letting people move on when their career prerogatives did not align with her goals. She discusses the inordinate amount of documentation that was required to be in compliance with the municipal government's policies and procedures when terminating an employee. She states, "It is hard to get in a full day's work as it relates to library work, and that to me is a real challenge and I resent that."[5]

Mary Bushing talks about the politics of administrating a library. She has worked in both public and academic libraries and identifies the same two types of politics in both institutions: capital *P* politics, which involves the administrative bureaucracies and established chains of command, but also small *p* politics, which entails responsibility to multiple constituents and the unstated powers within an organization:

> **What are the forces acting upon the library at any given time? So there are always frustrations because it isn't possible just to do the things that you see to be the best thing, but rather you have to work through the system.**
>
> **You have to learn how to be a diplomat. You have to learn how to compromise, even when you had rather just do what you know to be right.**[6]

Kent Middleton, a public librarian, also expresses frustration with being a low-level manager and the infighting among top management. Over the course of his career as a public librarian, he perceived the budget struggles as a constant battle between the library directors, who would attempt to gain the goodwill of the city council with little regard to the impact reduced services would have on the most needy patrons. He cynically states that perhaps the library directors believed if they cut costs in the short term, the council would support them with increased funding later on.[7] Later in the interview he relates how he would describe his job:

> **Well, I told friends and relatives that I was really more of a city bureaucrat during the time . . . I was a branch manager than I was a librarian. Because my time was almost completely taken up with staffing problems, purchasing problems, and customer complaints and I got very tired of that. So I don't miss any of that at all. When I was able to help customers directly, that was—that was always satisfying.**[8]

Karen Breen talks of losing what she loved by being promoted:

> **When I got to be head of children's services, I enjoyed it for quite a while, but then it became meetings and more meetings and more meetings. And all the things I loved the most, I lost—working with the kids, building a collection—I lost that.**[9]

Then she went to a conference where Margaret McElderry (a noted children's book publisher) was speaking. "And I listened to her and I turned to [the person seated next to me] and I said, 'I have just come to realize that I am never going to be Margaret McElderry. I need to pick what I want to do with my life and to really have a good time.'"[10] She left librarianship proper to become a successful consultant, staging workshops and conferences—working to inspire children's librarians who might also be bogged down with the minutiae of their jobs.

The art of collection development is a task that librarians report regretting the loss of in the process of being promoted to management. Kenneth Yamashita, a public librarian in California, specifically mentions how much he loved doing materials selection in his early career. While discussing the end of his career—which took place during a fiscal crisis and involved making difficult decisions about which branches to close, limiting hours of operation, and laying off staff—he reminisces about the joys of collection development during his early days. He enjoyed materials selection because of the impact it had on cultural communities that had not been well served. He reflects that collection development was an important responsibility that directly served the public. Though by most measures being the director of a large library system may involve much more responsibility, he *remembers* the act of collection development as being far more important.[11]

Jaye McLaughlin was a children's librarian who became a branch manager and then departmental manager for the Fort Worth Public Library in Texas. During her tenure collection development was first outsourced, then returned to a centralized staff for the entire system. She talks about this move away from the control of individual branch librarians with regret because it took the decisions and knowledge of new materials out of their hands. She discusses the attention that collection development was given during library school and how she truly enjoyed this facet of librarianship. Ms. McLaughlin relished the early part of her career when she really knew her branch's collection—because she had selected it. Collection development was satisfying because of the "immediacy of knowing what books were coming out," but that work was time consuming and "then something gave" and her attention was consumed with "dealing with all the problems with adult patrons as well as children's, and as well as planning your programs, as well as, you know, taking care of the pages and supervising." Looking back, she could not definitively say that outsourcing and then centralizing collection development adversely affected her library; however, she did miss that part of her early career. "But looking back . . . What difference did it really make? I don't know."[12]

Though there were aspects of moving into library administration that are bittersweet memories for Ms. McLaughlin, the overall experience of promotion into management was very rewarding. When asked if she ultimately enjoyed the increased responsibilities, she says, "Yes, much more . . . because I had more pull."[13] She discusses how her sense of the library mission was expanded when she became the advocate for children's services within the system administration of the large, northern Texas library. As an entry-level children's librarian and then a branch librarian, she had little experience with other departments. She enjoyed working with other departmental managers because they taught her about other aspects of librarianship from a systems standpoint: "I enjoyed managers' meetings and getting to know the other managers, because they all taught me a lot of things. Parts of the library that I wasn't aware of, you know, because we didn't have government documents in the children's department."[14] At one point she was cross-trained to work in the business library. This experience as part of a management team demonstrated to her that all the library divisions were interdependent. She came to appreciate each of the divisions: "[This] helped me respect a lot of the different librarians, and realize, you know, that we all have our specialties, so I could very much respect what they were doing. Therefore, I assumed I had that same respect."[15]

Elsewhere in the interview Ms. McLaughlin discusses how her new administrative status allowed her to develop a very gratifying skill and passion. As an early-career children's librarian, she was responsible for developing and executing weekly storytimes. The process of selecting a theme, finding the appropriate books, and doing a quick run-through of the stories consumed a great deal of time each week. But as a children's services division manager, she would only occasionally have to substitute for a vacationing or ill librarian's storytime. This gave her an opportunity to develop a repertoire of stories that she memorized. She began to tell stories instead of simply reading them. And this was far more rewarding, allowing her to really interact with her young audiences in a way that she never had time to do when it was a weekly chore.

> **When you are telling a story, you are telling them and looking into their eyes, and that story becomes much more immediate to them. Many storytellers will say it is not just the storyteller, but it is the audience and you are bringing it in and you are making something magical. If the audience isn't interested, it won't happen. If the storyteller isn't any good, it won't happen. When you are reading a**

> **book, the kids are focused on the pictures. When you are telling a story, they might create that picture in their mind.**
>
> **So it becomes a little bit more of an imagination and trying to understand, and—and it's not somebody else's idea of what it looked like. . . .**
>
> **The reason I didn't feel like I could learn the stories [before] was because I didn't feel like I had the time.[16]**

Nevertheless, Ms. McLaughlin's transition into management was not without trials. She relates, "I think there was an ongoing problem because I still really saw myself as being a children's librarian, so I didn't make that transition into management as well as perhaps my supervisors wanted me to do."[17]

Micki Freeny also missed storytime when she began to move up the administrative ladder. She says that she was always the storytime substitute for vacationing children's librarians because of her love of working with children, rather than simply managing librarians. Even as a library director, she enjoyed working the odd Sunday shift—much like Dr. Mears—in order to stay in touch with her institution's patrons because she loved public service. However, she also notes that as a manager she had the freedom to theorize and implement new ideas about children's services. As a manager she was able to take risks in developing programming that would have been impossible as an entry-level children's librarian. She reports that this power was exceptionally satisfying.[18]

Another librarian, Diana Collins, relates the joys of being a children's librarian and watching generations of kids grow up:

> **They're little sponges, they are open to learning, they want to learn, they want to be there, they want to be in the library! They love to come and sit on the story rug and hear the stories I love to share. And I love giving the child the perfect book and seeing them turn and say, "I want another one just like it." There's no greater words to a librarian.[19]**

But Ms. Collins laments the loss of that day-to-day contact with the kids when she became a library director. And then when the library outgrew its physical resources, all her time was consumed with a building project and fund-raising.

> **It became more of a fund-raising position, I was always raising money. I was the representative of the library in the community so I wasn't reading kids' books and placing books in hands or promoting large print or whatever to patrons, which was what I really liked. The people stuff is what I really liked, not the pleading for money from multiple organizations.[20]**

Children are not the only population that librarians reported missing as they climbed the administrative ladder. Both Ms. Collins and another public librarian, Karlan Sick, specifically mention their older patrons. Ms. Collins states, "I loved my seniors. The ninety-year-old gentleman in the little touring hat and the little convertible that roared up in front of the library to read the *Wall Street Journal* every day."[21]

Ms. Sick compares the two constituencies when asked what she missed about moving into management: "Seeing individual readers more often. [My library has] a large population of senior citizens and I found I really enjoyed working with them too. That was not dissimilar from working with children and teenagers because if they need help, you get up and help them. You don't just sit there."[22]

These nostalgic recollections filled with regret concerning advancement from entry-level positions—something most people would regard with enthusiasm—are particularly poignant because they are so unexpected. The next section addresses two issues involved with fiscal matters. Librarians discuss the struggle to support their institutions and their personal frustrations with salaries.

Funding and Compensation

The constant struggle for funding is another important element in the social memory of librarians. Fiscal challenges for their institutions, as well as regrets about their personal financial compensation, are found in many of the interviews. These are often the only elements of regret to be found in an interview about a librarian's professional life.

When asked about her biggest frustrations as a public librarian, Jeannette Larson first responds that she doesn't like to dwell on obstacles but would rather focus on solutions; however, she then volunteers that throughout the years of her career, there had been a constant struggle with the governing authorities over funding, and she wished they had consistently valued her mission as a library director. Because her funding was constantly in flux, programs and hours of operation were being adjusted—or eliminated—each year. She felt as though her patrons held only her responsible when they complained bitterly because their expectations for library service were not met, whereas the blame for reduced services truly belonged with the city and county administrators, who were inconsistent in their financial support.

However frustrating her experiences obtaining funding were, Ms. Larson uses humor: "Until the city manager has a child, they don't discover youth services—and then all of a sudden they are like, 'Oh my gosh, storytime! This is the greatest thing in the world.'"[23] She wishes there were other ways to get city administrators excited about the library and to ensure more consistent funding.

Also a public librarian, Diana Collins reiterated the importance of storytime as a funding tool: "That's kind of my philosophy, if I can hook them in story hour then I've got them for life."[24] She believes that a child who grew up in her storytime becomes her best advocate and an educated taxpayer, understanding the value of knowledge and libraries.

Ms. Collins describes her funding battles as a contest with the other government departments that were deemed essential (and rightly so), such as those providing police services and jails:

> **But I always felt like, well, what about the people that are doing their jobs right and want a library? . . . Instead of being a team that worked together to provide it, [the budgeting meetings] were adversarial and I hated that. I hated it. I hated it.**[25]

Ultimately Ms. Collins employs humor to describe a surprise financial gift. Earlier in the interview (and quoted earlier in this chapter), she had talked about relishing the time spent with her very youngest patrons *and the retired seniors*:

> **We had that little man that wore that little hat that drove up in his convertible at the age of whatever? When he died he left us half of his estate—it was over $100,000. So, who knew? I didn't know he had any money, but when he died he thought enough of us to leave us money. So that's the sort of thing that gets us through.**[26]

Connie Corson jokes about the administration's solution to a staffing shortage at her private girls' school library in New York City. The headmaster suggested she work with volunteers after her part-time clerk was let go during a budget shortfall. The library was considered a plum volunteer position, so there was no shortage of willing parents. At one point she had as many as thirty active volunteers. But managing all those volunteers consumed much more of her time than when she simply had a paid clerk—time that she should have spent with the students, the *raison d'être* of a school librarian. "My circulation system was totally messed up because they were doing the circulation and kindergartners had checked out, I mean, a totally inappropriate video or something for the—the upper schoolers."[27]

And she had to be careful not to hurt anyone's feelings, which made managing them even more difficult because these were powerful, important people. Only after several years of struggling was the clerk position restored.

Only one of the interview subjects had anything good to say about fund-raising. Irene Hoadley is the retired director of the Texas A&M library, an Association of Research Libraries (ARL) member. She believes that working hard to secure donations and grants brought prestige to the library and endeared it to the other departments. It leveled the administrative playing field within the university when the deans and president could see that she and her staff were contributing to the institution not only by providing ARL-level scholarship but also by helping to "pay their way."

> **It provided the opportunity for us to do some things that we would not have been able to do otherwise: the student computing area. We would not have had that, except for one individual who gave the money to do that. And being able to attract some of those kinds of things—some of those kinds of funds—was good. The other thing it did was, it gave the library a lot of visibility that it had not had before.**
>
> **Most people, if they thought of A&M—whether they were students there, or whatever their connection to the institution was—they have no real concept of a library. But once we got the mothers' clubs involved, and some of the other alumni groups, former students groups, then that gave more visibility to the library as an institution, and as a result, it's—some of that funding, and some of that recognition has continued to evolve and to develop. And that's only good for the institution.[28]**

The struggle to fund libraries is a perennial issue that directors and administrators negotiate with their governing bodies. Many expressed dismay at the process, wondering why they had to constantly remind funding authorities that the library's mission was important. But the inequity of personal compensation is a struggle that almost all the librarians interviewed referred to as simply "part of the job." Making money was not the reason people entered the profession. Andrew Hansen, after describing a thirty-year career in librarianship, says, "And I have often said I have never regretted becoming a librarian except every payday."[29] Diana Collins states, "You get to do something you love and you get paid for it! Minimally paid for it."[30]

Mary Bushing comments, "This is a fabulous way to earn a living. The salaries aren't great. You will never get rich, but it's a fabulous way to earn a living." Employing comedy, she goes on to say that there are other compensations besides the remunerative that make librarianship a personally valuable profession—such as having access to a great store of interesting anecdotes to share at cocktail parties. Then she uses irony: "if you ever attend any." Dr. Bushing ends this passage by stating the chief social memory of librarians: "you have to have a passion."[31]

Being passionate about librarianship is the compensation that is missing from the paycheck. In a previous chapter I related Micki Freeny's story about her bus ride home after getting her first job as a professional librarian. The bus driver asked her how much money she would be making, then exclaimed: "Nine thousand dollars? I make more than that! You have a master's degree and you're going to work for nine thousand dollars?"[32]

But not only are librarian salaries inequitable compared to those for similar professions requiring a master's degree, there are inequalities within the profession. Several children's librarians reported perceived slights from their fellow librarians in other departments as well as lower financial compensation. Rita Auerbach notes that children's librarian salaries often lagged behind those of their peers in public libraries, so that if you wanted to work with kids, it was more financially lucrative to work as a school librarian because those salaries were tied to the teachers' contract in her state.[33]

Karen Breen reiterates this viewpoint:

> **Never give up your children's librarian job. It's still the best thing. It's what you got into the business to do. For me, the frustration**

> **was children's librarians never get paid what everybody else gets paid. So they have to leave what they're doing to become better paid.[34]**

Many of the interviewees discuss their disenchantment with their salaries, especially when compared to those of other professional careers requiring a master's degree. But all the subjects reported personal rewards as career librarians that more than compensated them for their diminished earnings. The next section examines one possible reason that librarianship has never been a lucrative choice.

Sexism

The salary disparity can be attributed to sexism. Librarianship is considered a "pink-collar" vocation, and children's librarianship is especially considered a woman's career choice.[35] Connie Corson worked in the education department at the Museum of Modern Art, and she describes the mentality concerning human resources:

> **Our salaries were not as good as they were for men. I always felt that we were hired as if we were volunteers. . . . And there was an attitude in the museum that the women who worked there, most of them were usually volunteers. They were the wives of board members—for example, Board of Trustees members—and they did some very valuable work. They ran a Junior Council. They ran all kinds of educational programs and so on, but the assumption was that every woman must have a man who can afford for her to take a volunteer job. . . . Well, that was certainly not the case for me. I needed a job because I needed to earn money. My entire education, library school education, was all at my cost.[36]**

Library work as fit only for volunteers is a recurring theme in Ms. Corson's interview. When discussing a later job as a school librarian (see earlier in this chapter), she related the headmaster's insistence that she replace her clerk with parent volunteers.

Filomena Magavero's professional life began in the 1940s during World War II. She had studied to be a language teacher at Hunter College in New York City, but grew disenchanted with teaching as a career. Putting her language skills to use for the war effort, she applied to work for the Office of Censorship, translating intercepted international mail. But while waiting to be called for the Office of Censorship, she began work at the New York Public Library. After the war, she went to Columbia for a library degree.

Ms. Magavero began working at Fort Schuyler in 1949 and worked there until her retirement. Her story is about perseverance. She has always loved her library work; however, the conditions of her workplace were difficult. She was the only professional woman in a very male world of seamanship. She was not respected by many of the faculty because of her gender—they treated her like a clerk, or typist. Though the Fort was a naval academy, few of the senior staff possessed even a four-year baccalaureate degree. She was far more educated than most of her colleagues at the Fort, yet they insisted that she was simply a clerk. Why did she stay? Because she loved the work of librarianship and the mission of the Fort's library to preserve naval history.

Because she was a woman, Ms. Magavero was hired at the same pay rate as the clerks—even though she had her master's degree from Columbia and the majority of the rest of the faculty had only received the equivalent of a two-year "school ship" degree. She loved many aspects of her job as a librarian, but the entrenched sexism of the all-male military college left her with many bitter memories:

> **And here I am, with much more education, and I was hired as a clerk. Now I questioned that of the librarian at the time, you know. I thought, "Why should I be in the clerical line?" He said, "Well,**

there's nothing I could do," you know, "this is the way it is," and, you know, I accepted. . . .

But I didn't realize that these people [laughs] would start treating me like a clerk, and always did, and were mean-spirited about it, you know, they really were. I had no restroom facilities. I had to walk two blocks outside of my office. In the winter I had to put on a coat, a hat, and boots to go and wash my hands [laughs]. And these men had—what they used to call them "heads"—in the Navy, a bathroom is a "head." They had heads one on top of the other on two separate levels in the Fort, and I had to walk two blocks outside, you know, and it was a little ridiculous. . . . One of—I call—I shouldn't even call them professors, they really weren't [laughs], but they would come over and throw a piece of paper at me and say, "Type this," you know, and I would say, "But, I don't type"—you know [laughs], that kind of thing.[37]

Ms. Magavero relates this story with a tragic tenor but is quick to say that she loved the work. She also enjoyed a special place in the hearts of many of the sailor students who went through the Fort. As the only faculty woman, in addition to teaching scores of students how to conduct research in the library, she was the Fort Mother to hundreds of young men away from their homes and families for the first time in their lives. She stayed within the clerical pay scale for thirteen years before the salary inequity was addressed. "I'm not going to let these guys run me out of here, just because they want to treat me as [a] clerk."[38]

But Ms. Magavero also is quick to use comedy to discuss her regrets, especially when relating the story of how she ultimately got a women's washroom in the same building with the library:

It was only because one day we had—we received a gift—and if anybody knows anything about gifts that you get from somebody's attic or basement, it was moldy, and dusty. And I think I had to put on my hat and my coat to go to the restroom, really just to

wash my hands, maybe four or five times that day, because the material I was working with was so dirty. So that by late afternoon, when I made maybe the fourth trip, I just walked into the admiral's office—because in those days the president of the Maritime College was not called "president," he was called "admiral" all the time. So I walked into the admiral's office, with my black hands [laughs], and I held them in his face, and I said, "You know I've made this trip here, maybe four times today, just to wash my hands," and he saw I was practically in tears, so he said, "Sit down, Fil."

And so I explained what happened. I said, "You know we don't have a washroom in the Fort for the women." And I said, "That's awful." So he said, "Okay, I'll do something about it." So the next day . . . he came over, he took me into the men's head, and he said, "What if we covered the urinals?" [Laughs] So I said, "I don't care what you do. You could leave them just the way they are, just put a latch on the door, and when I'm in there, I'll lock myself in." So he said, "No, we'll fix it up, and this will be your Ladies' Room."

And he did. So I finally got a ladies' room, after two years. After two years, I finally got a ladies' room [laughs], which was good [laughs].[39]

I loved my job. My job was so—was just so fantastic. I went there as a cataloger, but I took over the duties of government documents. I took over the duties of periodicals. I was the first periodicals librarian. I collected archival material, wherever I could find it. I did all of that. It was so—it was so varied, it was so interesting. I just loved it. And I thought, you know, "I'm not going to let these guys run me out of here, just because they want to treat me as [a] clerk." So the way I handled it was to just ignore them; I just totally ignored them. I had nothing to do with them. I didn't have a single friend on the faculty, and I didn't care, it didn't bother me because I was busy with my work, and happy with my work.[40]

This interview is special in many ways. Its creator, Jane Brodsky Fitzpatrick, worked with Ms. Magavero and Richard Corson at the Fort Schuyler library. This oral history interview was recorded in 2005 for the StoryCorps project of the Library of Congress. Using this interview as her focus, Ms. Fitzpatrick then wrote a thoughtful book about women in librarianship titled *Mrs. Magavero: A History Based on the Career of an Academic Librarian.*[41] When Ms. Fitzpatrick learned of the *Capturing Our Stories* project, she inquired whether her StoryCorps recording could be shared with my project, and Ms. Magavero gave her consent. Ms. Fitzpatrick went on to record and contribute the interviews with Connie and Richard Corson for my project as well.

It is with comedy that many of the other social memories involving sexism are handled. Valerie Feinman remembers a double standard that benefited women employees of one of her earliest libraries. She was paid an extra stipend when she began working on the bookmobile because the act of climbing into the cab of the truck was deemed unladylike if performed wearing a skirt. Because these women were asked to wear pants, they were paid an extra $3 so that their pants could be dry-cleaned.[42]

Bill Mears remembers his experience as a male librarian in a female-dominated institution, recounting a funny story about required knowledge that was not included in his library school curriculum:

> **At the university, one of the little things that I knew how to take care of was when the men's urinals ran over because the handle got stuck. I knew how to go in and unstick that. And they would always call me and say, you know, "Dr. Mears, can you go to the restroom [laughter] and fix it—." And . . . I would always think, walking there to do that job, "This is what I went and got a PhD for? [Laughter] So I could . . . ." But anyway—I like every part of being a librarian. I like even that part. I like every part of being a librarian.**[43]

Echoing Ms. Magavero's experience as the only professional woman at an all-male institution, Ms. Feinman reports that she was one of only two women in an academic science department. "There was one lady, in the dean's office, and there was me." She laughs as she shares a perquisite of the arrangement: she married one of the physics doctoral students.[44]

Earlier in her interview, Ms. Feinman discusses the limited vocational opportunities for women in the middle of the twentieth century:

> **Something that most of you watching this don't understand—or won't—is that women in Canada had very few options open to them in the '50s. If they became a teacher, they had to retire when they were pregnant. They could become a nurse, if they didn't get married. They could try to go on to graduate school, but they were not allowed into architecture schools, medical schools, law schools, etc. I had a good friend who wanted to become a lawyer. Her father was a chief justice and he got her into law school. No one would hire her and she worked in her father's office. And that was the truth of life in 1950, '55, '59—when I graduated from college.**[45]

These regrets are a part of the social memory of our profession. They are shared across most of the interviews; however, our subjects make it very clear that they do not regret their choice of career. The benefits of being a librarian have always outweighed the regrets. This vocation has been rewarding because it has allowed librarians to be of service in their communities in a meaningful way, day after day. They helped people.

NOTES

1. Kathy Kaya, interview by Mary Bushing, June 6, 2010, video recording, transcript, A. Arro Smith "Capturing Our Stories" Oral Histories Program, 2005-2012 97/1/70, American Library Association Archives at the University of Illinois, Urbana-Champaign, 10:25.
2. Ibid., 23:06.

3. Bill Mears, interview by Stephanie Langenkamp and Arro Smith, February 29, 2007, video recording, transcript, A. Arro Smith "Capturing Our Stories" Oral Histories Program, 2005-2012 97/1/70, American Library Association Archives at the University of Illinois, Urbana-Champaign, 11:53.
4. Andrew Hansen, interview by A. Arro Smith, July 13, 2009, video recording, transcript, A. Arro Smith "Capturing Our Stories" Oral Histories Program, 2005-2012 97/1/70, American Library Association Archives at the University of Illinois, Urbana-Champaign, 10:43.
5. Sheila Ross Henderson, interview by Cathy Prazak, April 15, 2010, video recording, transcript, A. Arro Smith "Capturing Our Stories" Oral Histories Program, 2005-2012 97/1/70, American Library Association Archives at the University of Illinois, Urbana-Champaign, 12:40.
6. Mary Bushing, interview by Kathy Kaya, June 6, 2010, video recording, transcript, A. Arro Smith "Capturing Our Stories" Oral Histories Program, 2005-2012 97/1/70, American Library Association Archives at the University of Illinois, Urbana-Champaign, 09:33.
7. Kent Middleton, interview by Gustavo Soto, November 12, 2008, video recording, transcript, A. Arro Smith "Capturing Our Stories" Oral Histories Program, 2005-2012 97/1/70, American Library Association Archives at the University of Illinois, Urbana-Champaign, 20:16.
8. Ibid., 55:44.
9. Karen Breen, interview by Kristy Raffensberger, June 4, 2008, audio recording, transcript, A. Arro Smith "Capturing Our Stories" Oral Histories Program, 2005-2012 97/1/70, American Library Association Archives at the University of Illinois, Urbana-Champaign, 14:31.
10. Ibid., 14:58.
11. Kenneth Yamashita, interview by A. Arro Smith, June 28, 2010, video recording, transcript, A. Arro Smith "Capturing Our Stories" Oral Histories Program, 2005-2012 97/1/70, American Library Association Archives at the University of Illinois, Urbana-Champaign, 25:13.
12. Jaye McLaughlin, interview by A. Arro Smith, April 16, 2011, video recording, transcript, A. Arro Smith "Capturing Our Stories" Oral Histories Program, 2005-2012 97/1/70, American Library Association Archives at the University of Illinois, Urbana-Champaign, 47:41.

13. Ibid., 36:34.
14. Ibid.
15. Ibid., 35:16.
16. Ibid., 18:36.
17. Ibid., 05:27.
18. Micki Freeny, interview by A. Arro Smith, July 10, 2009, video recording, transcript, A. Arro Smith "Capturing Our Stories" Oral Histories Program, 2005-2012 97/1/70, American Library Association Archives at the University of Illinois, Urbana-Champaign, 12:03.
19. Diana Collins, interview by Jessica Kirkland, November 16, 2008, video recording, transcript, A. Arro Smith "Capturing Our Stories" Oral Histories Program, 2005-2012 97/1/70, American Library Association Archives at the University of Illinois, Urbana-Champaign, 04:38.
20. Ibid., 06:29.
21. Ibid., 05:10.
22. Karlan Sick, interview by Kristy Raffensberger, May 19, 2008, audio recording, transcript, A. Arro Smith "Capturing Our Stories" Oral Histories Program, 2005-2012 97/1/70, American Library Association Archives at the University of Illinois, Urbana-Champaign, 25:14.
23. Jeannette Larson, interview by Janssen Bradshaw, Allison Steeger, Kimberley Francisco, and Timothy Arnold, November 15, 2008, video recording, transcript, A. Arro Smith "Capturing Our Stories" Oral Histories Program, 2005-2012 97/1/70, American Library Association Archives at the University of Illinois, Urbana-Champaign, 19:07.
24. Collins, 53:23.
25. Ibid., 47:48.
26. Ibid., 27:56.
27. Connie (Cornelia) Corson, interview by Jane Brodsky Fitzpatrick, August 3, 2009, audio recording, transcript, A. Arro Smith "Capturing Our Stories" Oral Histories Program, 2005-2012 97/1/70, American Library Association Archives at the University of Illinois, Urbana-Champaign, 32:24.
28. Irene Hoadley, interview by Joan Heath and Arro Smith, April 27, 2010, video recording, transcript, A. Arro Smith "Capturing Our Stories" Oral Histories

Program, 2005-2012 97/1/70, American Library Association Archives at the University of Illinois, Urbana-Champaign, 20:34.

29. Hansen, 16:23.

30. Collins, 35:53.

31. Bushing, 46:30.

32. Freeny, 05:11.

33. Rita Auerbach, interview by Kristy Raffensberger, June 11, 2008, audio recording, transcript, A. Arro Smith "Capturing Our Stories" Oral Histories Program, 2005-2012 97/1/70, American Library Association Archives at the University of Illinois, Urbana-Champaign, 11:33.

34. Breen, 29:52.

35. D. J. Grimes, "Marian the Librarian—The Truth behind the Image," in *Discovering Librarians: Profiles of a Profession*, M. J. Scherdin, ed. (Chicago: Association of College and Research Libraries, American Library Association, 1994), 3–11; P. Wilson, *Stereotype and Status: Librarians in the United States* (Westport, CT: Greenwood Press, 1982).

36. C. Corson, 17:11.

37. Filomena Magavero, interview by Jane Brodsky Fitzpatrick, November 3, 2005, audio recording, transcript, A. Arro Smith "Capturing Our Stories" Oral Histories Program, 2005-2012 97/1/70, American Library Association Archives at the University of Illinois, Urbana-Champaign, 07:40.

38. Ibid., 13:26.

39. Ibid., 19:11.

40. Ibid., 13:30.

41. Jane Brodsky Fitzpatrick, *Mrs. Magavero: A History Based on the Career of an Academic Librarian* (Duluth, MN: Library Juice Press, 2007).

42. Valerie Feinman, interview by Sarah Albert, June 29, 2008, video recording, transcript, A. Arro Smith "Capturing Our Stories" Oral Histories Program, 2005-2012 97/1/70, American Library Association Archives at the University of Illinois, Urbana-Champaign, 12:09.

43. Mears, 16:48.

44. Feinman, 16:43.

45. Ibid., 06:20.

Chapter 5

HELPING PEOPLE

THE SOCIAL MEMORY OF LIBRARIANSHIP AS EXPRESSED through these oral history interviews can be summed up as a desire to help people find the information they needed and to make an impact on the lives of patrons. The specifics of this impact depended on the nature and type of librarianship practiced. School and children's librarians devoted their careers to instilling an essential love of reading. Catalogers across library types worked to build an efficient infrastructure for knowledge. Public services librarians worked to provide frontline access to information for their communities and to cultivate a love of lifelong learning. Academic librarians served their faculties and students pursuing advanced research. No matter the individual discipline within librarianship, a single vision of what these librarians did emerges from the interviews: they helped people.

As I began processing the interviews for this study, I had in mind specific elements of the social memory to "look for" in the individual recordings. (These elements were cliché, stereotype, nostalgia, and regret.) But I also gave myself permission to broaden the research parameters if other elements became evident. Very soon after beginning the process of methodically analyzing the interviews, I found that almost all the interviews contained a "What I did" statement that often summed up the entire interview. The following extracts come from these "What I did" statements.

Many of the interviewees fondly related how their patrons had thanked them years—sometimes decades—after having helped them with a research paper or introducing them to a favorite author. Jeannette Larson recalls having two different people who had been library volunteers as children thank her for their introduction to the library. They were both getting their master's degrees in library science. The mother of another child declared that her daughter still talks about the time, over eighteen years before, that Ms. Larson took her to a library conference to meet children's book authors. Ms. Larson believes that perhaps teaching is the only other career "where you really have people come back and say . . . you really made a difference for me."[1]

Kathryn Kaya relates a similar story. She was an academic librarian and describes her reference work as more than simply handling referrals and providing answers—she developed relationships with her college students. Over the course of their matriculation and education, many would return to her reference desk because they had developed a rapport, and they knew they could trust her with their research problems. She specifically recalls a local contractor: "Every time he sees me, he thanks me for helping him get his master's degree—because he was my student."[2] And he graduated over thirty years ago.

Robert Gaines, also an academic librarian, expresses similar memories of helping students learn to become competent researchers. He describes this as the most fulfilling part of his career. Mr. Gaines seems amazed that he has been blessed with this gift of being able to help people. "You have changed their life in some way by providing them with the information they need. That is always very fulfilling. And it can happen tens of thousands of times in a library career."[3]

Ninfa Trejo came to public librarianship rather late in life as a second career, but she found it very rewarding because of the interactions she had with people. She describes library work as not about books but about "lives."[4]

Sheila Henderson discusses a strategy she used in Georgetown, Texas, to reach out to kids who were not library patrons:

> **But you see, you can—you can do things that will change people's behavior. Behind the library in Georgetown was an old building. It was a shotgun house that they eventually made into a museum for the African American community. That was where the kids that were catching the bus would gather in the mornings. Boys and girls, and all ages, and they would be so rowdy. Okay, I started arriving early and I would have a bag of candy. Now did they need candy? No. [Laughter]**
>
> **But I had a bag of candy and I would go and I would sit on the porch, and they would have to talk to me and share their homework with me and any problems that they had or whatever, and I would hand out candy. And that got to be a regular event. So you know, whatever you can do to affect a positive outcome for not just your patrons that walk in the door but your potential ones as well.[5]**

Filomena Magavero was the only woman working at a naval school. She describes stories of her work with young men, many of whom had never been away from home before becoming cadets. In the middle part of the twentieth century, there were no mental health professionals on campus for these boys:

> **You know I really—I think I helped a lot of them . . . I knew so many of them well, they worked in the library, or I knew them because I worked with them on research problems, or, you know, whatever. So they would come and they would tell me their sad tales, and I tried to help them as much as I could, and that was another thing, that was another one of my jobs [laughs].[6]**

Ms. Magavero was their librarian, but also their motherly advisor.

Arlene Luster shares similar memories as a military librarian stationed at several overseas military bases. She also had homesick boys in a strange country who appreciated her as a confidante and valued her ability to find books for them to read that reminded them of home.

Diana Collins remembers watching her storytime children grow up and helping them with their middle school homework, then their high school research projects. She describes the preschool and elementary children as "little sponges," saying they are just completely open to learning and they want to be in the library. She loved listening to their interests and finding picture books: "I love giving the child the perfect book and seeing them turn and say, 'I want another one just like it.' There's no greater words to a librarian."[7] Eventually she would have the pleasure of working with the children of those children. Her strategy has been to "hook them in story hour, then I've got them for life. . . . And be taxpayers—and educated taxpayers who understand the value of knowledge and how to find knowledge."[8]

Peggy Richwine relates a story about her enthusiasm for the library. She was a science bibliographer at an academic library. One morning she had been assigned the task of giving a tour of the library to a group of folks. She went downstairs and found a group of people in the lobby and proceeded to give them a tour of the library—all four floors. At the conclusion of the tour, back down in the lobby, they thanked her. And then her associate pointed out another group of people waiting patiently. *They* were the people who had come for the tour. "And my colleagues, they were just cracking up. Because they couldn't believe I was so enthusiastic, that I'd just grabbed the first person that came in the door, and gave 'em a tour."[9]

Pat Tuohy discusses the balance that must be struck between administering the library efficiently and pursuing the ultimate goal for the library. She began her career as a public librarian and is now the retired director of CTLS (Connecting Texas Libraries Statewide, formerly known as the

Central Texas Library System). In this latter role her perspective is broad, and she works to inspire individual librarians to remember their goals:

> **Oh, you know, it's so easy to be distracted by the crazy bureaucracy we find ourselves in, and libraries cannot—librarians cannot—avoid bureaucracy. We are part of it. We are integral to it. [We must] keep reminding ourselves: You're doing this for people—the people you care about—the public in a generic way, but also people in a small way. Like the kids that live down the block, the senior citizens you may know. It's really hard to, with all the bureaucratic crap that comes down, but the reason you're there is to serve people. And you're doing the Lord's work with helping them connect with information: reading, viewing, whatever it is that enriches their lives in a positive way. And that's what you have to keep reminding yourself, that there's a reason you're putting up with all of this madness. That the end result of your efforts are worthwhile and people are going to benefit and they may never know your name, but you may be planting a memory in a child about how they were helped finding something that expanded their life and their vision.**
>
> **You hear this from successful people, you hear them say, I remember when I went into the Brooklyn Public Library—or the Honolulu Public Library—and got what I needed and it had an impact. It had an impact on their life, a positive one. They will not remember your name or your face, but they'll remember what you did for them. And keeping that in mind—that that's the real reason you're there—is the hardest thing to do, but the most important. Or you will go crazy having to put up with the craziness.**[10]

Many other interviewees also referred to the magic of helping people—remember Jennifer John Patterson's "magic helper" from chapter 3. Dr. Irene Hoadley described her role as an administrator as one of fostering relationships that help professionals learn to help library patrons. Karen Breen discussed her role on the Caldecott Medal Selection Committee as ultimately helping children find the best picture book that year. Rita Auerbach and Karlan Sick both summed up their careers as helping children discover the joys of reading. Richard Corson talked about how his abilities to help people with research increased exponentially over his career—about how his knowledge was cumulative. Helping one college student research a topic would increase his skills so that he was an even better librarian for the next student. Helping people was what these librarians did.

NOTES

1. Jeannette Larson, interview by Janssen Bradshaw, Allison Steeger, Kimberley Francisco, and Timothy Arnold, November 15, 2008, video recording, transcript, A. Arro Smith "Capturing Our Stories" Oral Histories Program, 2005-2012 97/1/70, American Library Association Archives at the University of Illinois, Urbana-Champaign, 06:45.
2. Kathy Kaya, interview by Mary Bushing, June 6, 2010, video recording, transcript, A. Arro Smith "Capturing Our Stories" Oral Histories Program, 2005-2012 97/1/70, American Library Association Archives at the University of Illinois, Urbana-Champaign, 18:14.
3. Robert Gaines, interview by Anne Marie Taber, August 15, 2008, video recording, transcript, A. Arro Smith "Capturing Our Stories" Oral Histories Program, 2005-2012 97/1/70, American Library Association Archives at the University of Illinois, Urbana-Champaign, 25:31.
4. Ninfa Trejo, interview by Sarah Ann Long, June 27, 2008, video recording, transcript, A. Arro Smith "Capturing Our Stories" Oral Histories Program, 2005-2012 97/1/70, American Library Association Archives at the University of Illinois, Urbana-Champaign, 07:08.
5. Sheila Ross Henderson, interview by Cathy Prazak, April 15, 2010, video recording, transcript, A. Arro Smith "Capturing Our Stories" Oral Histories Program, 2005-2012 97/1/70, American Library Association Archives at the University of Illinois, Urbana-Champaign, 49:02.

6. Filomena Magavero, interview by Jane Brodsky Fitzpatrick, November 3, 2005, audio recording, transcript, A. Arro Smith "Capturing Our Stories" Oral Histories Program, 2005-2012 97/1/70, American Library Association Archives at the University of Illinois, Urbana-Champaign, 29:46.
7. Diana Collins, interview by Jessica Kirkland, November 16, 2008, video recording, transcript, A. Arro Smith "Capturing Our Stories" Oral Histories Program, 2005-2012 97/1/70, American Library Association Archives at the University of Illinois, Urbana-Champaign, 04:54.
8. Ibid., 53:23.
9. Peggy Richwine, interview by Kacy Allgood, August 27, 2008, video recording, transcript, A. Arro Smith "Capturing Our Stories" Oral Histories Program, 2005-2012 97/1/70, American Library Association Archives at the University of Illinois, Urbana-Champaign, 52:46.
10. Patricia Tuohy, interview by Jessica Kirkland, June 17, 2009, video recording, transcript, A. Arro Smith "Capturing Our Stories" Oral Histories Program, 2005-2012 97/1/70, American Library Association Archives at the University of Illinois, Urbana-Champaign, 55:02.

Chapter 6

THE COLLECTIVE MEMORY OF LIBRARIANSHIP

SO, AT THE END OF THE DAY, AFTER INTERVIEWING THIRTY-FIVE retired librarians, what do we have? What have we learned?

The most surprising repeated element among all the narratives—and poignant lesson, for me—was that of promotion regret. As a late-midcareer librarian myself, I can learn from these stories of administrators and library directors. They long to experience the practical librarianship that involves helping patrons, conducting research, sitting on the floor for storytime, or (in my case) just cataloging a book and making the decision of where to classify it.

One of my personal mentors, Dr. Bill Mears, found a way to schedule in a balance of administrative work with shifts on the reference desk—but he could do this because he was the director, the decision maker. Micki Freeny also told us how she always insisted on being the first substitute for storytime even when she was the library director. But many of the other interviewees expressed regret that moving up the administrative ladder meant losing touch with the very aspects of librarianship that had attracted them to the profession in the first place. They did enjoy the power and prestige—and the additional salary—but they missed their entry-level duties and working with the public.

End-of-career librarians remember their decision and motivations to join this profession. Many remembered their first childhood library experiences. They have regrets and nostalgia for their earliest days as librarians, before technology radically changed the profession and before they advanced into management positions. The subjects interviewed do not regret becoming librarians, but they did express regrets about their financial compensation, and many also struggled to secure stable funding for their institutions.

The *Stories* interviews also demonstrate a perception among librarians that work with children is less important than work with adults. Many of the children's librarians interviewed recalled memories of inferiority, lack of respect, and lack of financial compensation compared to their peers. Karen Breen implores her interviewer:

> **Never give up your children's librarian job. It's still the best thing. It's what you got into the business to do. For me, the frustration was children's librarians never get paid what everybody else gets paid. So they have to leave what they're doing to become better paid.**[1]

Rita Auerbach, Diana Collins, Jaye McLaughlin, Karlan Sick, and Micki Freeny all shared memories of heartache when leaving behind their entry-level children's librarian jobs to pursue administrative careers within their library systems. And one librarian, Connie Corson, related her story of indecision about taking a school library position—which she really wanted—because she was unsure how her former peers at an academic library and at the Museum of Modern Art would perceive her move. These interviews do show that there is a perception within the social memory that children's librarianship is less important and, therefore, less prestigious.

At the outset of this study, I expected to find stories about how library work evolved as technology developed and stories involving the library stereotype. These stories are well represented here. But I was surprised by the internal use of cliché that separates the technical services staff from the public services staff. I was also amused to find so many "accidental librarians," especially so many whose first choice of career was in classroom education.

My favorite stories from the archive discuss not only interviewees' library careers but also how they chose the career—and how they felt about choosing this career. I also really love when the interviewees were honest about the drawbacks of the career choice. This straightforwardness tells the history of librarianship that is not to be found in any other source.

Filomena Magavero's recording is a potent reminder of midcentury sexism. But she also clearly enjoyed her work, despite the hostile environment.

Besides the outstanding Magavero interview, I found Pat Tuohy's, Mary Bushing's, Jeannette Larson's, and Sarah Long's interviews charming in their candor and brimming with personal insight. Ms. Tuohy's work with many central Texas public libraries as the director of a regional consulting and advocacy organization gave her a firsthand perspective of how small libraries originate, grow, and flourish. Both Dr. Bushing and Ms. Larson worked as consultants after their retirement as librarians, and both shared a broad view of the profession from their outlook as trainers. Ms. Long is an ALA past president, so she was also able to share a catholic view of librarianship. All four of these women are public speakers in their professional capacities. They were not shy about sharing their thoughts about librarianship in their oral history interviews.

Valerie Feinman's recollections were deeply personal and often simply hilarious. She recounted the limited occupational opportunities for women in the 1950s, especially those interested in the sciences. With wit and charm she crafted a career that satisfied her desires for intellectual stimulation, and she shared her story in a most appealing way. The interview with Bill Mears included great personal stories—including his childhood memory of desiring a sex instruction book that was kept behind the circulation desk. Micki Freeny's interview was poignant, especially when discussing the unintended consequences of technological innovation at her library.

For me, the takeaway messages are succinct:

> No matter how high administratively I may climb, keep one foot on the main floor of the library—with the patrons.
>
> Embrace technology, but do not let it alienate. Make my staff be a living and breathing conduit between our patrons and the virtual world.
>
> Know the stereotype, and embrace the elements of it that are good. (I would love to be able to rattle off *The Song of Hiawatha* like Katharine Hepburn in *Desk Set.*)
>
> Be careful about employing library clichés to dismiss library work that is not our forte. Words matter. (And catalogers do have feelings.)
>
> Work hard to ensure that our profession is respected and paid a fair wage, but also know that it is a calling that has its own rewards.

NOTE

1. Karen Breen, interview by Kristy Raffensberger, June 4, 2008, audio recording, transcript, A. Arro Smith "Capturing Our Stories" Oral Histories Program, 2005-2012 97/1/70, American Library Association Archives at the University of Illinois, Urbana-Champaign, 29:54.

Part II

HOW TO CAPTURE STORIES

Oral history is different. . . . it tells us less about events as such than about their meanings.

—Alessandro Portelli

IN THIS SECOND PART OF THE BOOK, I DISCUSS THE THEORY AND METHodology that guided the *Capturing Our Stories* project. The first section of chapter 7 discusses the methodology of oral history. The second section examines the theories I borrowed from the emerging field of memory studies to interpret the interviews in the *Capturing Our Stories* project. Both of these sections include a literature review that may be of interest only to researchers. Please feel free to skip these sections unless you are working on a formal, scholarly project.

The final chapter includes advice for conducting an oral history project, including a checklist. I share practical advice on how to approach an interview and avoid the mistakes I made while conducting the *Capturing Our Stories* project. The book concludes with a meditation on the nature of oral history work—why it is important, and how it makes the interviewer a better human being.

Chapter 7

A PRIMER ON ORAL HISTORY THEORY AND METHODOLOGY

Successful doctoral research in the social sciences is the unique combination of two parts of a puzzle. The parts are theory and methodology. They provide a new solution to an existing puzzle—which may, or may not, substantiate earlier solutions to the puzzle. The new combination of *this* theory with *that* method is what a successful doctoral candidate strives for.

Theories are just theories. They are ideas about how we interact, or how nature works. When we apply a theory, we must choose a method—or methodology. The methodology is the tool we use to test the theory. Some methods are quantitative: they count stuff. Others are qualitative: they are more complicated than just counting stuff. (A qualitative researcher might sit down with thirty-five individual librarians and ask them to tell the story of their vocation.)

An Introduction to the Methodology: Oral History

The interviewees in this archive are librarians from a variety of professional backgrounds; they retired from school libraries, academic libraries, public libraries, military libraries, medical libraries, and a prison library. The interviews have been conducted by many different volunteer interviewers, themselves librarians or library school students—some of whom have been formally trained in oral history methodology, but many of whom were not. The *Capturing Our Stories* website includes a "Training Documents" section that provides volunteers with instructions on the process—notably, to come prepared with a few basic questions, but to allow the subjects to guide the content and "tell their own story."[1] Though some historians might blanch at this lack of rigor, the chief motivation has been to "capture" the stories within a reasonable time frame by coordinating volunteer resources. In many respects, the very parameters of the project allow a degree of freedom in the collection of the interviews that would not be appropriate in another setting.

Although it takes training and practice to collect a successful life history using the methodology,[2] an oral history interview limited to the professional life of a librarian—and conducted by a fellow librarian—can be successfully executed by a volunteer. Several factors make this approach possible: librarians are well educated, have an appreciation for history and preservation, and, for the most part, are fond of talking about their profession.

Oral history is the methodology of choice for this project because a "bottom-up" account of the profession was desired: real, practicing librarians discussing their careers as opposed to a historian's account of librarianship.

HISTORY OF THE METHOD

Rebecca Sharpless notes in her historiography of oral history that the practice is far from new:

> Practitioners of the modern oral history movement enjoy contemplating its ancient origins, sometimes pointing out with glee that all history was oral before the advent of writing. From the Greek side come the historians Herodotus, who employed first-person interviews

> in gathering information for his account of the Persian wars in the fifth century BCE, as well as Thucydides, who interrogated his witnesses to the Peloponnesian War "by the most severe and detailed tests possible." In the Zhou dynasty of China (1122–256 BCE), the emperor appointed scribes to record the sayings of the people for the benefit of court historians. Africanists point to the *griot* tradition in recording history, in which oral traditions have been handed down from generation to generation.[3]

Though the methodology may have been popularized in the 1960s and 1970s, one of its first large-scale projects was conducted during the Great Depression. The Works Progress Administration (WPA) documented a corpus of slave narratives from a population of Americans quickly disappearing.[4] Over 2,300 firsthand accounts were collected from 1936 through 1938.

Oral history interviews have been the basis for many notable works addressing the African American civil rights movement, including the *Autobiography of Malcolm X*; *Freedom Riders: 1961 and the Struggle for Racial Justice*; *Voices of Freedom: An Oral History of the Civil Rights Movement from the 1950s through the 1980s*; and *All God's Dangers: The Life of Nate Shaw*.[5]

Appalachian lives and folkways were profiled in the enormously popular Foxfire series in the 1970s beginning with *The Foxfire Book: Hog Dressing; Log Cabin Building; Mountain Crafts and Foods; Planting by the Signs; Snake Lore, Hunting Tales, Faith Healing; Moonshining; and Other Affairs of Plain Living*.[6] This book sold more than 100,000 copies in its first month of publication.[7]

Studs Terkel's best-selling books are another example of this method's acceptance in popular culture, including *Working: People Talk about What They Do All Day and How They Feel about What They Do* and *Hard Times: An Oral History of the Great Depression*.[8]

In this century, oral history is beginning to assert itself on the Internet—notably, the Library of Congress's Veterans History Project,[9] the

Oral History of the U.S. House of Representatives,[10] StoryCorps,[11] and the ACT UP Oral History Project.[12] Many of the WPA slave narratives are included in the Library of Congress's site, *Born in Slavery*.[13]

Modern oral history was contingent on the development of recording equipment—first, wire audio recording and then tape recording, introduced in 1948.[14] Michael Frisch laments the fact that many well-conceived oral histories are lost or ignored simply because the tapes, and even possibly the transcripts, end up stored in an archive and forgotten.[15] An example of this problem is an entry from the Austin (Texas) Public Library in the 1986 American Library Association publication, *A Directory of Oral History Tapes of Librarians in the United States and Canada*.[16] The *Directory* shows an oral history of Annie Campbell Hill, 1876–1979, conducted in 1977. She was the head reference librarian for many years at the University of Texas. The recording is twenty minutes long, and there is a transcript. However, there is no entry in the Austin Public Library's or the Austin History Center's online catalog for this interview. It is either uncataloged or lost.

Frisch reports that a new era of oral history is being developed with digital technologies. This twenty-first-century technology makes the creation of oral history sharp and clear with high-definition video. Streaming technology on the Internet makes the dissemination of oral history much more accessible, and digitized oral history transcripts make research more facile and precise with robust full-text searching. Frisch states:

> These considerations help define the threshold on which we stand: digital technologies are opening new ways to work directly and easily with audio and video documents. Oral history audio and video can now be placed in an environment in which rich annotation, cross-referencing codes, and other descriptive or analytic "meta-data" can be linked to specific passages of audio-video content. By searching or sorting by means of these reference tools, the audio-video materials themselves—not the transcribed text version—can be searched,

> browsed, accessed, studied, and selected for use at a high level of specificity. Indeed, with many of the emerging tools for providing such access, users and researchers themselves can mark, assess, analyze, select, and export meaningful audio and video passages for a range of customized research, presentational, and pedagogic uses.[17]

Frisch posits that the new technological media for oral history usher the promise of the method even closer to fruition—namely, that the histories are freed even further from editorial intervention.

Frisch's prediction was proved in my own project. The entire corpus of unedited recordings used to create this work is digitally archived using the GLIFOS rich-media platform. GLIFOS is a web-based technology that enables a viewer to listen to the actual, unedited interviews while the transcript scrolls automatically.[18] Most of the interviews also include streaming video, so the viewer can listen to the voices of the narrators, see their expressions, and read the transcripts, which are synched with the recording. The transcripts may be keyword searched, and many include a table of contents. The use of this state-of-the-art technology is but one aspect of this original research project. The website for the *Capturing Our Stories* project is hosted by the School of Information at the University of Texas at Austin (www.ischool.utexas.edu/~stories/), and archival copies of all the interviews are part of the American Library Association Archives at the University of Illinois at Urbana-Champaign. Both the recordings and the transcripts are available through Illinois's online catalog.

Paul Thompson in 1978 noted, "The challenge of oral history lies partly in relation to [the] essential social purpose of history. This is a major reason why it has so excited some historians, and so frightened others."[19] Another seminal oral historian writes, "Oral sources tell us not just what people did, but what they wanted to do, what they believed they were doing, and what they now think they did."[20] Many oral history proponents point out the singular subjectivity of this practice that sets it apart from traditional history.

However, modern oral history is different from oral tradition: It is a narrator's account of her own experience, told in her own voice. It is recorded using an objective (technological) medium. It is unedited. The technology of portable recording devices has made oral history possible, which explains why this methodology is fairly recent.[21]

Oral history is also different from journalism. Though oral history is facilitated by an interviewer, the interviewer allows the narrator to tell her own story. A good oral history interviewer only prompts the subject to continue or to expand on the narrator's own tangents.[22] Whereas journalism is a process of culling sources, editing, and corroborating, oral history is an intimate exposition of a personal memory with only minimal intervention by the interviewer.

These issues are addressed in Alessandro Portelli's chapter, "What Makes Oral History Different" in his seminal work, *The Death of Luigi Trastulli, and Other Stories.* He begins this chapter by stating the obvious, that "oral sources are *oral* sources."[23] This concise statement stresses the preeminence of the recording of the narrator's voice, without the intervention of a transcriber or reporter—or even written words.

Though most modern people in the developed world are literate, few people have the facility or gift to write well enough that their words produce a satisfying story or narrative. Paul Thompson notes that "the overwhelming majority of published autobiographies are from a restricted group of political, social, and intellectual leaders."[24] Good writers, whether they are historians, creative writers, or memoirists, are rare; however, many people—whether literate or not—are able to *tell* a good tale. Portelli begins his discussion by stating the obvious to clearly set the parameters of his work. He has asked people to *tell* their stories. He knows that when the recordings get transcribed, then edited and—in the case of his English-speaking readers—translated, much is lost:

> This is one reason why I believe it is unnecessary to give excessive attention to the quest for new and closer methods of transcription. Expecting the transcript to replace the tape for scientific purposes

> is equivalent to doing art criticism on reproductions, or literary criticism on translations. The most literal translation is hardly ever the best, and a truly faithful translation always implies a certain amount of invention. The same is true for transcription of oral sources. . . . The tone and volume range and the rhythm of popular speech carry implicit meaning and social connotations which are not reproducible in writing.[25]

The English Popular Memory Group meditated on this insight, noting that "a knowledge of the past and present is also produced in the course of everyday life"; however, this "common sense" of history is rarely recorded, since it lives "in everyday talk and in personal comparisons and narratives."[26] In this way oral history is able to capture what may be easily overlooked and lost.

Alessandro Portelli's own work examines Italian labor relations among steelworkers in Terni and a misremembered murder during a strike, as well as the events surrounding the mass execution at Fosse Ardeatine in Rome during the Nazi occupation.[27] In *The Order Has Been Carried Out: History, Memory, and Meaning of a Nazi Massacre in Rome*, Portelli (2003) writes:

> One of the differences between oral and written sources is that the latter are documents while the former are always acts. Oral sources are not to be thought of in terms of nouns and objects but in terms of verbs and processes; not the memory and the tale but the remembering and the telling. Oral sources are never anonymous or impersonal, as written documents may often be.[28]

Paul Thompson notes in *The Voice of the Past:*

> In all these fields of history, by introducing new evidence from the underside, by shifting the focus and opening new areas of inquiry, by challenging some of the assumptions and accepted judgments of his-

> torians, by bringing recognition to substantial groups of people who had been ignored, a cumulative process of transformation is set in motion. The scope of historical writing itself is enlarged and enriched; and at the same time its social message changes. History becomes, to put it simply, more democratic.[29]

CRITICISM OF ORAL HISTORY

Oral history is celebrated in progressive circles because of its ability to bring out and preserve the silences of traditional history. The methodology of oral history comes from a desire to document the vernacular events and social lives of everyday people—people who would never be the subject of a traditional biography.[30] It is often used to preserve a record of the activities of "subaltern" groups—people whose work or existence undermines the hegemony of the dominant culture, whose thoughts and ideals are silenced by the majority.[31]

But what of the criticism that these tales and stories are just that: tales and stories? Many traditional historians bristle when oral history is contemplated as a method because they doubt its credibility. Here Portelli defends the method by pointing to a different credibility:

> Oral sources tell us not just what people did, but what they wanted to do, what they believed they were doing, and what they now think they did. . . . The importance of oral testimony may lie not in its adherence to fact, but rather in its departure from it, as imagination, symbolism, and desire emerge. Therefore, there are no "false" oral sources.[32]

This change in emphasis has been noted as a paradigm shift in history circles, embracing postmodernist and feminist theory and moving away from positivist notions about history and objectivity.[33] Portelli continues:

> Traditional writers of history present themselves usually in the role of what literary theory would describe as an "omniscient narrator." They

> give a third-person account of events of which they were not a part, and which they dominate entirely and from above (above the consciousness of the participants themselves). They appear to be impartial and detached, never entering the narrative except to give comments aside, after the manner of some nineteenth-century novelists. Oral history changes the writing of history much as the modern novel transformed the writing of literary fiction: the most important change is that the narrator is now pulled into the narrative and becomes a part of the story.[34]

This is not just a grammatical shift from the third to the first person, but a whole new narrative attitude. The narrator is now one of the characters, and the *telling* of the story is part of the story being told.

Paul Connerton discusses the difference between traditional history and oral history in his chapter "Social Memory" in *How Societies Remember.* In order to justify the apparent lapses of historical fact found in oral histories, he notes that the subjects are not members of the elite—and so they should not be bound by a chronology or historical authority imposed by the dominant culture. He continues, "The historian will only exacerbate the difficulty if the interviewee is encouraged to embark on a form of chronological narrative. For this imports into the material a type of narrative shape, and with that pattern of remembering, that is alien to that material. In suggesting this, the interviewer is unconsciously adjusting the life history of the interviewee to a preconceived and alien model. That model has its origin in the culture of the ruling group."[35] Though his caveat about oral history—that it will "produce another type of history: one in which not only will most of the details be different, but in which the very construction of meaningful shapes will obey a different principle"—is an interesting observation about oral history in general, it may not always be applicable, as when the narrators are well educated and are familiar with the historical canons of the cultural elite.[36]

My subjects, well-educated professional librarians, were also keenly aware of how history is created. Other than historians, librarians may be the population most familiar with issues of historiography. A majority of the content of most libraries involves history. Librarians spend a great deal of time deciding which histories to include in their collections—and they must be prepared to defend their decisions. Librarians are aware of what constitutes good history. The majority of librarians are students of history. They know how a history is constructed; therefore, the oral history interviews that they participated in as subjects are often well crafted, even relative to a traditional history. The parameters of the project also contribute to accuracy: the *Stories* subjects are discussing their professional lives, so their memories are organized by periods of education and work for specific institutions. So Connerton's caveat about oral history is largely inapplicable to this study of librarian oral histories.

In his book *A Shared Authority: Essays on the Craft and Meaning of Oral and Public History,* Michael Frisch relates an illuminating story about the power of this research technique. The *New York Times* had commissioned the author to research and write an article about unemployment in Buffalo, New York, in the mid-1970s using oral history methodology. Frisch was excited to use this progressive methodology in a way that would demonstrate its value to a nonacademic audience: the readers of the *Times.* He was aware of the issues of class, hegemony, and interpretation that occur in what he calls "History—capital *H*" and how they can be mitigated by using oral history—lowercase *h*.[37]

Frisch discusses the triangulation that takes place between the interviewer (recording History), the narrator, and the narrator's memories (oral history with a little *h*). Being conscious of this triangulation—and guarding against the biases of the interviewer's interpretation (History)—is the key to a successful oral history.[38]

Frisch's interviews collected for the *Times* article were successful and honest; however, the project began failing when the work had to be edited for mass consumption by his team of researchers. One of the things that makes oral history different from journalism is the fact that it is the *narrator's* story, told in her own way, including (and excluding) what *she* deems important.[39] Conscientious editing may be possible in order to present a cogent and concise project, but it must be done very carefully. Frisch reports that he and his team became leery at the outset of the process when confronted with the *Times*' parameters for the story; however, they worked hard to present a true account of the subjects' interviews, sans overt interpretation.

But the *Times* editors imposed an additional layer of interpretation. They were in the business of selling newspapers. They desired an article—a story—that their readers would *enjoy,* along with Sunday morning bagels and coffee. They wanted poignancy! This is where the very careful attention to triangulation—the relationships between the interviewer, the oral history, and the narrator—became so muddled that the story was no longer "true." Here is an example of Paul Thompson's comment become manifest: "The challenge of oral history lies partly in relation to [the] essential social purpose of history. This is a major reason why it has so excited some historians, and so frightened others."[40] The *Times*' editors were not happy with Frisch's research—it terrified them.

This perversion of the "story" by the *New York Times* is an example of what Linda Tuhiwai Smith would refer to as colonizing research except, instead of Buffalo's underclass, her thesis involves Western "positivists" imposing their own cultural assumptions and mores on indigenous peoples.

Her controversial work, *Decolonizing Methodologies: Research and Indigenous Peoples,* lays bare the epistemological heart of the issue within Western science: there are non-Western ways of knowing, communicating, and comprehending—even remembering. Her thesis details many ways that positivist science has impoverished indigenous cultures through overt colonization and subtle misunderstandings of the very nature of their wisdom and lifeways. Smith describes how the West has failed to understand many basic tenets of indigenous culture not only because of language barriers but also because of a failure to understand that different notions of time, space, and gender role create wholly incompatible worldviews, even when the words are successfully translated. She maintains that centuries of misguided studies conducted by arrogant and insensitive interlopers have poisoned the entire notion of research for many non-Westerners. Smith's work is a manifesto calling on indigenous peoples to cease cooperating with first-world scientists and to begin a program of research that is sympathetic to their own goals, values, and modes of knowing.[41]

Oral history methodology is a Western tool that can help to amend the "colonizing" histories of the past by letting indigenous peoples tell their own stories in their own voices. Smith would argue that all oral histories need to be created by—and for—indigenous peoples; however, even if conducted by outsiders, the methodology holds promise to ameliorate many of the inequities of past Western research when it is conducted in a fashion respecting the mores and customs of the culture. Smith describes several issues that the Western researcher often misunderstands. These include personal agency, the role of the community, privacy mores, hierarchies, and the aforementioned notions of time, space, and gender. What Smith has to teach all researchers, no matter their setting or agenda, is that a successful program must include reflection and the knowledge that not all research subjects "think" or express themselves the way scientists schooled in the Western canon of thought might expect.

Oral history methodology captures meaningful and sublime information in a manner that more traditional research methods may miss. It is clearly different from traditional data collection techniques: it is different from "capital *H*" history, biography, journalism, or surveys.

The narrator's product of an oral history interview is different from the story that narrator would tell among friends and family, and it is different from the autobiography that she might write. The narrative shared among friends and family (her social networks) contains implicit references that are known—and not made explicit.[42] The autobiography—if it were ever to be written—would be a careful and guarded, self-edited creation: possibly a work of literature. The successful oral history interview is blessed with two advantages: the interviewer is a sympathetic "outsider," and the interview is a spontaneous dialogue. Anna Green in her work on collective memory describes it in this way:

> There are differences between the fixed, literary written form of life narrative, and the fluid, interactive and often more ambivalent dialogue that is generated in the oral history interview. . . . Reminiscing with one's contemporaries . . . writing an autobiography, and responding to an oral historian are all very different mnemonic contexts.[43]

The spontaneous dialogue produces a far more "true" story than if a narrator were taking the time to consider, write, and edit. In other words, this "triangulation" that Frisch speaks of is beneficial: it is part of the magic of this methodology.

An Introduction to Memory Studies as Theory

The concept of social memory is an important aspect of understanding and appreciating this collection of oral histories. My main theorists are Maurice Halbwachs, a French sociologist who was a protégé of Durkheim and who lived from 1877 to 1945, and Paul Connerton, a British sociologist, still living. Halbwachs and Connerton view society as the most powerful force in shaping memory and history.

The field of memory studies is a relatively new discipline that combines theory and method from a variety of scholarship. In many ways, it is simply a way to examine historical and sociological experience through a lens focusing on human memory, particularly collective memory.[44] Though memory studies scholarship is not primarily devoted to oral history, it supplies sublime but powerful theory to understand the content and context of oral history.

COLLECTIVE MEMORY

Maurice Halbwachs posits that all individual memories are "kept" via the medium of our social groups. Personal history is organized and remembered through our interactions with others, also remembering. In his work titled "The Social Frameworks of Memory," published in *On Collec-*

tive Memory, he describes three main "collectives" that almost all people share in their unique positions as social creatures: the family, religious life, and social class.[45]

Librarians share an initial social framework through their experience in a graduate school cohort. They then share a professional life that may include networking within associations and at annual conferences. But they also share a collective memory of their citizenship, their "place" within a social class, and even their gender.

Paul Connerton's work in memory studies also explores society as the most powerful force shaping memory and history. Connerton divides memory into three types: personal, cognitive, and habit. Personal memories "refer to those acts of remembering that take as their object one's life history. We speak of them as personal memories because they are located in and refer to a personal past," whereas a cognitive memory holds objective information or refers to events that the subject did not personally experience.[46] A "habit memory" is the "capacity to reproduce a certain performance. Thus remembering how to read or how to write or how to ride a bicycle is in each case a matter of our being able to do these things, more or less effectively, when the need to do so arises."[47] This taxonomy of memory is also found in Maurice Halbwachs's notions of collective memory; however, Connerton's theory expands on Halbwachs's by including bodily gestures, manners, and clothing to find the nexus of memory in the corporeal world of society.

Pierre Nora has detected a change in how people remember in the modern era. He believes this shift is due in part to the contemporary turn to memorialize and "make" what we call *history*. Before the professionalization of history—and the printing press—all history was social or collective memory. Nora, who is French, summarizes many of his ideas about modern historiography in an English-language article in *Representations* titled "Between Memory and History: Les Lieux de Mémoire."[48] He believes the advent of professional historians has led to certain events of the past becoming fixed by their memorialization as artifacts in books and monuments, which is counter to past ways of remembering:

> Memory is life, borne by living societies founded in its name. It remains in permanent evolution, open to the dialectic of remembering and forgetting, unconscious of its successive deformations, vulnerable to manipulation and appropriation, susceptible to being long dormant and periodically revived.[49]

Nora worries that the accumulation of monuments—what is known throughout the field of memory studies by the French term *les lieux de mémoire,* or "sites of memory," in homage to his exhaustive work—is profoundly changing the way we remember, perhaps cluttering our memories with static "sites" that take the place of the more natural and organic memories of our past.

Halbwachs and Nora set the stage for a discussion of the place of memory, whether it can be termed an individual memory, or a collective memory as perpetuated through our social networks, or a "site of memory," an artifact of history-making in the modern sense.

INDIVIDUAL MEMORY AND CRITICISM

Although the field of memory studies has matured and Halbwachs's notion of collective memory has served as its taproot, some scholars have noted a theoretical problem that especially manifests itself when employing oral history methodology: though it is useful to regard all memories as existing in realms of the collective memory, the fact is that each memory belongs to—resides within and issues from—an individual. Anna Green discusses this reality in her *Oral History* article, "Individual Remembering and 'Collective Memory.'" She warns researchers to not minimize individual memory and the capacity for subjects to be reflective and critical:

> Oral historians need to re-assert the value of individual remembering, and the capacity of the conscious self to contest and critique cultural scripts or discourses. Rather than seeking to fit oral narratives to pre-existing cultural representations or psychoanalytic templates,

> would it not be more fruitful for oral historians to explore those points of conflict and rupture in people's lives that create confrontations with discourses of power?[50]

Susan Crane has also tackled this issue in "Writing the Individual Back into Collective Memory." Like Nora, she discusses modern memory in terms of a "culture of preservation we have inherited." Her solution is to create a "middle term" to represent the balance between historical memory (Nora's *lieux de mémoire*) and collective memory: "historical consciousness." This term is taken from another scholar, Amos Funkenstein. In this way, Crane relocates the "collective back in the individual who articulates it—the individual who disappeared in the occlusion of personal historical consciousness by the culture of preservation."[51] Crane posits that the creation of historical artifacts does freeze the collective memory in a point in time but that the agency of the act is through an individual accessing the collective. And each time an individual recalls and articulates a memory from the collective, she does so as an individual negotiating her own unique path through that collective. "I am suggesting that historical research is a lived experience that the self-reflexive historian consciously integrates into collective memory."[52] This is the "historical consciousness" that balances historical memory and collective memory.

These ideas about social memory—or collective memory—formed the theoretical basis for this study, but to give the research some parameters, Dr. Roy and my dissertation committee identified four additional theoretical elements to "look for" in the interviews. They are regret, based on the work of Janet Landman; ideas of what constitutes—and causes—nostalgia, taken from Renato Rosaldo; and cliché and stereotype, drawn from the work of Jan Vansina.

REGRET AND NOSTALGIA

Narrative and oral history are strongly tied to emotive responses as the subjects voice feelings such as regret in the midst of nostalgia. Renato Rosaldo has written about nostalgia in a way that may have relevance to a study involving oral history methodology. Here is his etymological introduction to the term:

> To "us," feelings of nostalgia seem almost as "natural" as motor reflexes. How can one help but feel nostalgic about childhood memories? Don't all people in all times and in all places feel nostalgia? Yet even the history of the concept in Western Europe reveals the historical and cultural specificity of our notion of nostalgia. Far from being eternal, the term *nostalgia* (from the Greek *nostos*, "to return home," and *algia*, "a painful condition") dates from the late seventeenth century when it was coined to describe a medical condition. The term described, for example, a pathological homesickness.[53]

Although Rosaldo goes on to describe nostalgia as "idealized fantasies designed to gloss over violence and brutality"[54] by imperialist colonizers, the kernel of his argument is that women and men reflect on their pasts in ways that promote the vision of their lives in which they wish to believe.

A similar notion is found in Alon Confino's article, "Collective Memory and Cultural History: Problems of Method." Confino invites us to view memory "as an outcome of the relationship between a distinct representation of the past and the full spectrum of symbolic representations available in a given culture."[55] Similarly, Lewis Coser writes that Maurice Halbwachs explores social memory with a "presentist approach. . . . He argues that the beliefs, interests, and aspirations of the present shape the various views of the past."[56]

In a multidisciplinary work on the concept of regret, Janet Landman examines many aspects of remorse. She begins her study by identifying regret as the only alternative to nostalgia that exists within memory:

> The only *past* we much like is the sentimental past of nostalgia, a cozy place furnished with golden oldies, retro watches, and vintage vehicles. Otherwise, we keep our distance. For to reflect on the real, unsentimentalized past is to open oneself up to regret, feeling sorry

> about past mistakes, misfortunes, and missed opportunities. In shunning the past, we shun regret.[57]

Later in the book she writes, "Though memory does not always evoke regret, regret is frequently associated with memory."[58]

Landman uses an expansive variety of methods and disciplines to discuss regret, including philosophy, ethics, psychology, and mathematical models of economic decision theory, but her chief inspiration comes from a typology of literary analysis, dividing novels, plays, and poetry into four categories: comedy, tragedy, romantic, and ironic.[59] Using this literary taxonomy, she is able to identify different types of regret and their responses. These gradations of regret expose useful subtlety when studying oral histories.

CLICHÉ AND STEREOTYPE

Both Connerton's social memory and Rosaldo's notions of nostalgia are influenced by ideas about stereotype and cliché. Jan Vansina discusses the importance of "listening" for the cliché in his chapter titled "The Message Expresses Culture." He describes cliché as "deliberate and purposeful simplifications" that "must be interpreted symbolically because they cannot be accepted as they stand."[60]

The word *stereotype* has been used in the social sciences since the 1920s. Pauline Wilson writes about the origin of the term in her *Stereotype and Status: Librarians in the United States*: "*Stereotype* is a term taken from printing. When a body of type is set, a mold is made of it. The mold is then used to cast a metal plate. The plate is the stereotype."[61] She notes that in a 1922 publication Walter Lippmann used the word to describe the process by which people not fully informed reach conclusions based on generalizations. "Stereotypes prevail because they are useful, even necessary. They are a way of organizing learning, a way of organizing experiences with certain groups of people. . . . Once learned, they become a social reality or social fact. They are real although they are not palpable. They become 'pictures in our heads.'"[62]

Well known and well documented are the stereotypes and clichés that are part of the popular culture notions of librarians and librarianship.[63] Vansina's theory and guidelines for identifying cliché within narratives provide a powerful tool to examine oral histories of the profession to expose subtle meanings about the nature of librarianship.

Combining the Theory with the Method

When considered with Halbwachs's notions of collective memory, Jan Vansina's ideas about cliché and stereotype provide a unique study of librarianship. It is cleaved from the traditional history of the profession by its emphasis on individual subjectivity—the hallmark of oral history work—and uses the lens of memory studies to identify the social bedrock that the profession shares.

The collective memory of librarianship begins with participation in a graduate school cohort. Then the common experience of librarianship extends into a professional life that may include networking within associations and at annual conferences. Outside their professional lives, many will share a common experience as members of the "middle" socioeconomic class.[64] From these networks, each individual will develop ideas of what it is to be a "librarian." These notions may include ideas about scholarly disposition and personality—and even highly specific notions about what kind of personality fits the individual roles that librarians may inhabit (e.g., children's librarian, cataloger, director, reference librarian).

But Halbwachs's and Connerton's social memory work is purely theoretical. Neither offers a practical methodology to ascertain the collective or social memory. Here is where we bring in theory from the methodology of oral history. Paul Thompson and Alessandro Portelli, among many other practitioners, show how oral history captures subjective and implicit elements of life that may be ignored and undocumented by traditional forms of history.[65] These oral historians provide not only a theory of why these stories are "true" and important to preserve but also a methodology to capture them.

The stepping-stone that bridges Halbwachs's collective memory theory and oral history method is found in Alessandro Portelli's work interviewing a cohort of Italians who witnessed a murder, recounted in *The Death of Luigi Trastulli*, and in *The Order Has Been Carried Out: History, Memory, and Meaning of a Nazi Massacre in Rome* as well as in Jan Vansina's work, *Oral Tradition as History*. Portelli's oral history work concentrates on gathering versions of the same story and finding the essence of the social memory by collating repeating elements and comparing them to more traditional historical documents to expose inconsistencies. He does not suggest that the social memory is wrong; it is simply the organic memory that is shared by the participants. Although the remembered circumstances of Mr. Trastulli's death—even the year of his death—may completely differ from archived newspaper accounts, Portelli does not suggest that the social memory is incorrect; the social memory is simply a different truth than the history constructed by the journalists of the time. Portelli argues that the social memory trumps the traditional history because it is the social memory that influences the current population of Terni, Italy.

Portelli is able to extract the social memory from a cohort by conducting individual oral history interviews and collating the shared memories. His methodology inspired this *Stories* research project, providing an approach to examine the professional lives of retired librarians and to identify elements of the social memory that is shared by the profession.

Librarians at the Intersection of Memory Studies Theory and Oral History

The master's degree in library science, acquired at an American Library Association–accredited graduate school, may be the only collective memory that *all* librarians truly share. Library work can be very diverse. There are public, school, academic, law, medical, and corporate libraries—just to name a few. Within each type of library there are a multitude of professional positions—for example, reference, cataloging, programming, children's services, collection development, acquisitions, and administration. Some graduates never step into a traditional library, instead using their bibliographic skills to collect, index, and administer databases. Each type of library has its own professional association and conferences—and within each association are individual "round tables" and focus groups. There is a society (and a very specific social framework and collective memory) for everyone involved with librarianship; however, each professional librarian has attended an ALA-accredited graduate school. This accreditation imposes a core body of knowledge deemed essential for being a modern "librarian."[66] Some of the professional standards that are indoctrinated into future librarians through this process include bibliographic control, reference best practices, collection development, and "philosophy, principles, and ethics of the field."[67]

The *Stories* interviews demonstrate that library school memories are a recurring trope. The experience of earning a master's degree in library science may be the most compelling shared memory in the collective consciousness of the profession. Though this memory's recurrence across the corpus of interviews may be biased—because it is a frequent lead question by interviewers attempting to establish an easy rapport with the narrator—it may be the most pervasive aspect of our professional collective memory because the act of attending library school was the genesis of our careers as librarians.

One historical issue that has affected modern librarianship is the very nature of information—there is just more of it. The print publication industry alone has experienced phenomenal growth in this century. In the years 2002–2008 new book titles grew an amazing 126 percent.[68] To stretch a concept from Pierre Nora, each of those books could be considered a "site of memory," or, in his coinage, *les lieux de mémoire*.[69] Nora actually posits that collective memory is dying because of the culture of preservation: "Archives, museums, memorials, anniversaries, and histories needed to be created by modernity because spontaneous collective memory has ceased to function."[70] Whatever the case may be, it is the modern librarian who must preserve, index, and make accessible each individual "site" in this explosion of memory.

Fortunately, there are new technologies to assist in the bibliographic control of this "explosion" of information. The memories of this dramatic increase of information sources may be the most important to document in this project. The librarians retiring in the twenty-first century learned the tools of their trade when computers at the library were found only in the pages of the science fiction books in the stacks. Librarians trained in the 1960s and 1970s learned to expertly manage three-by-five-inch cards fed into a typewriter. Each book would be represented by at least three surrogate cards in the catalog drawers: author, title, and subject. Each additional subject, added author, or series statement required another surrogate card to be created and filed. Halbwachs's *On Collective Memory* would have required the creation and filing of six cards. Most librarians did not do the actual typing and filing, but they had to have expert knowledge of these tasks in order to train and supervise their clerical staff. The circulation of said materials was another equally daunting task: keeping track of who borrowed what and when it was due.

Technology liberated librarians (and their staff) from the most time-consuming clerical tasks; however, it did not change the "science" of bibliographic control. Technology simply made it far more efficient and precise. These are powerful memories that many of the narrators share. "Let me tell you about the first computer we got . . ." is a recurring line in the oral histories of the *Stories* project.

However liberating the computer was in daily tasks of librarianship, the labor and time savings were quickly consumed by entirely new mediums of information: databases, Gopher, Fetch, electronic discussion lists, and, ultimately, the Internet. These same technologies also made self-publishing far more viable, resulting in even more "traditional" (bound paper) items necessary to organize and preserve. The social memory of late-twentieth-century librarianship is dominated by the changing nature of our work brought about by the challenges and opportunities of technology.

Historians of technology, journalists, and information science researchers have done a fine job documenting each step in the march of computer automation and processing. What the narrators of the *Capturing Our Stories* project do differently is describe their individual—personal—experiences with the new tools of the library trade. These oral histories provide a "bottom up" story of what it was like to discover the power of computer processing, and how library work changed and adapted. This is a social memory that only this generation of librarians can share. The individual memories are different, but a powerful collective memory emerges from the corpus.

The "So What?" Question

As I prepared my dissertation, I attended a number of my more advanced colleagues' dissertation defenses in my department, the School of Information at the University of Texas. The dean of our school, Dr. Andrew Dillon, is always present at these events, and I found that he posed the same question to each doctoral candidate: "So what?"

I worked very hard to have a ready answer to the "So what?" question: Oral history projects have been focused on librarians and librarianship before the *Capturing Our Stories* project. This is documented in the 1986 ALA publication, *A Directory of Oral History Tapes of Librarians in the United States and Canada.*[71] A Google search reveals many, many more librarian oral history projects—some currently underway. But none of these are as extensive as the *Stories* project, nor as accessible. The *Stories* project breaks ground because it represents a diverse cross-section of librarians from many parts of the country. It is original because it uses the state-of-the-art technology available to the School of Information at the University of Texas to deliver its content to anyone with a broadband Internet connection. These oral histories are available to be viewed, studied, and enjoyed—unlike past projects that are limited by the technological constraints of previous eras.

My work is original because it takes theories about collective memory from Halbwachs and a methodology from Alessandro Portelli and applies them to a cohort of librarians at the end of their careers. They tell their stories of ushering librarianship into the twenty-first century using tools they never dreamt possible when they began their careers. In addition to letting the narrators tell their own stories, this research has applied interpretive tools to bring out implicit meanings through the analysis of stereotype and cliché, nostalgia, and regret.

So what? This research is important because it examines a generation of librarians that is quickly disappearing. It lets them speak for themselves to document what they consider important about their careers and professional lives. It lets them share their memories of how librarianship made radical changes because of technological innovations. These are important stories. They deserve to be shared and archived. Alongside the capital-*H* Histories and encyclopedia articles about millennial librarianship, this research allows future scholars to literally see and hear individual librarians describe how they practiced the art and science of librarianship. This work distills their recollections into a social memory that represents the entire cohort.

NOTES

1. A. Arro Smith and Loriene Roy, "Training Documents," *Capturing Our Stories: Developing a National Oral History Program of Retiring/Retired Librarians*, www.ischool.utexas.edu/~stories/.
2. D. M. DeBlasio, *Catching Stories: A Practical Guide to Oral History* (Athens, OH: Swallow Press, 2009).
3. Rebecca Sharpless, "The History of Oral History," in *Handbook of Oral History*, T. L. Charlton, L. E. Myers, and R. Sharpless, eds. (Lanham, MD: AltaMira Press, 2008), 19.
4. D. Campos, "Slave Narratives from the Federal Writers' Project 1936–1938: Stories as a Catalyst for Historical Comprehension," *Black History Bulletin*

69(2), (2006), 8–14; A. B. Govenar, *African American Frontiers: Slave Narratives and Oral Histories* (Santa Barbara, CA: ABC-CLIO, 2000).

5. Malcolm X and Alex Haley, *The Autobiography of Malcolm X* (New York: Grove Press, 1965); R. Arsenault, *Freedom Riders: 1961 and the Struggle for Racial Justice* (New York: Oxford University Press, 2006); H. Hampton, S. Fayer, and S. Flynn, *Voices of Freedom: An Oral History of the Civil Rights Movement from the 1950s through the 1980s* (New York: Bantam Books, 1990); Nate Shaw and T. Rosengarten, *All God's Dangers: The Life of Nate Shaw* (Chicago: University of Chicago Press, 2000).
6. E. Wigginton, *The Foxfire Book: Hog Dressing; Log Cabin Building; Mountain Crafts and Foods; Planting by the Signs; Snake Lore, Hunting Tales, Faith Healing; Moonshining; and Other Affairs of Plain Living* (Garden City, NY: Doubleday, 1972).
7. T. Sitton, G. L. Mehaffy, and O. L. Davis, *Oral History: A Guide for Teachers (and Others)* (Austin: University of Texas Press, 1983).
8. Studs Terkel, *Working: People Talk about What They Do All Day and How They Feel about What They Do* (New York: Pantheon Books, 1974); Studs Terkel, *Hard Times: An Oral History of the Great Depression* (New York: Pantheon Books, 1970).
9. Library of Congress, *Veterans History Project Collection, circa 1914–2007*, www.loc.gov/vets/vets-home.html.
10. "Oral History of the [U.S.] House [of Representatives]," http://oralhistory.clerk.house.gov.
11. StoryCorps, *StoryCorps Collection*, www.storycorps.net.
12. ACT UP, *ACT UP (AIDS Coalition to Unleash Power) Oral History Project*, www.actuporalhistory.org/.
13. Works Progress Administration and Federal Writers' Project, *Portraits of African American Ex-Slaves from the U.S. Works Progress Administration, Federal Writers' Project Slave Narratives Collections*, http://memory.loc.gov/ammem/snhtml/snhome.html.
14. Sharpless, "The History of Oral History."
15. Michael H. Frisch, "Oral History and the Digital Revolution: Toward a Post-Documentary Sensibility," in *The Oral History Reader*, R. Perks and A. Thomson, eds. (New York: Routledge, 2006).

16. D. C. Dale and American Library Association, *A Directory of Oral History Tapes of Librarians in the United States and Canada* (Chicago: American Library Association, 1986).
17. Frisch, "Oral History and the Digital Revolution," 103–4.
18. Jessica Kirkland, A. Arro Smith, and Loriene Roy, "Capturing Our Stories and GLIFOS: Rich-Media Video," *Electronic Library* 28(5), (2010), 650–56.
19. Paul Thompson, *The Voice of the Past: Oral History* (New York: Oxford University Press, 2000), 3.
20. Alessandro Portelli, *The Death of Luigi Trastulli, and Other Stories: Form and Meaning in Oral History* (Albany: State University of New York Press, 1991), 50.
21. B. W. Sommer and M. K. Quinlan, *The Oral History Manual* (Lanham, MD: AltaMira Press, 2009).
22. DeBlasio, *Catching Stories.*
23. Portelli, *The Death of Luigi Trastulli,* 46.
24. Thompson, *The Voice of the Past,* 28.
25. Portelli, *The Death of Luigi Trastulli,* 47.
26. Popular Memory Group, "Popular Memory: Theory, Politics, Method," in *The Oral History Reader*, R. Perks and A. Thomson, eds. (New York: Routledge, 2006), 45.
27. Portelli, *The Death of Luigi Trastulli;* Alessandro Portelli, *The Order Has Been Carried Out: History, Memory, and Meaning of a Nazi Massacre in Rome* (New York: Palgrave Macmillan, 2003).
28. Portelli, *The Order Has Been Carried Out,* 14.
29. Thompson, *The Voice of the Past,* 8–9.
30. C. S. Brown, *Like It Was: A Complete Guide to Writing Oral History* (New York: Teachers and Writers Collaborative, 1988).
31. R. Young, *Postcolonialism: A Very Short Introduction* (New York: Oxford University Press, 2003).
32. Portelli, *The Death of Luigi Trastulli,* 50–51.
33. Richard Perks and A. Thomson, "Critical Developments: Introduction," in *The Oral History Reader*, R. Perks and A. Thomson, eds. (New York: Routledge, 2006).

34. Portelli, *The Death of Luigi Trastulli*, 56–57.
35. Paul Connerton, *How Societies Remember* (New York: Cambridge University Press, 1989), 19.
36. Ibid., 22.
37. Michael H. Frisch, *A Shared Authority: Essays on the Craft and Meaning of Oral and Public History* (Albany: State University of New York Press, 1990), 59–60.
38. Portelli, *The Death of Luigi Trastulli*.
39. DeBlasio, *Catching Stories;* J. R. Tisdale, "Observational Reporting as Oral History: How Journalists Interpreted the Death and Destruction of Hurricane Audrey," *Oral History Review* 27(2), (2000), 41–65.
40. Thompson, *The Voice of the Past*, 3.
41. Linda Tuhiwai Smith, *Decolonizing Methodologies: Research and Indigenous Peoples* (London: Zed Books, 1999).
42. Maurice Halbwachs, *On Collective Memory* (Chicago: University of Chicago Press, 1992).
43. Anna Green, "Individual Remembering and 'Collective Memory': Theoretical Presuppositions and Contemporary Debates," *Oral History* 32(2), (2004), 40–41.
44. J. K. Olick and J. Robbins, "Social Memory Studies: From 'Collective Memory' to the Historical Sociology of Mnemonic Practices," *Annual Review of Sociology* 24(1), (1998), 105.
45. Halbwachs, *On Collective Memory*.
46. Connerton, *How Societies Remember*, 22.
47. Ibid., 22–23.
48. Pierre Nora, "Between Memory and History: Les Lieux de Mémoire," *Representations* 26 (1989), 7–24.
49. Ibid., 8.
50. Green, "Individual Remembering," 42–43.
51. Susan A. Crane, "Writing the Individual Back into Collective Memory," *American Historical Review* 102(5), (1997), 1375.
52. Ibid., 1382.
53. Renato Rosaldo, "Imperialist Nostalgia," *Representations* 26 (1989), 109.

54. Ibid.
55. Alon Confino, "Collective Memory and Cultural History: Problems of Method," *American Historical Review* 102(5), (1997), 1391.
56. Lewis A. Coser, "Introduction," in *On Collective Memory*, M. Halbwachs and L. A. Coser, eds. (Chicago: University of Chicago Press, 1992), 25.
57. Janet Landman, *Regret: The Persistence of the Possible* (New York: Oxford University Press, 1993), 6.
58. Ibid., 204.
59. Ibid., 247.
60. Jan Vansina, *Oral Tradition as History* (London: James Currey, 1985), 139.
61. Pauline Wilson, *Stereotype and Status: Librarians in the United States* (Westport, CT: Greenwood Press, 1982), 3.
62. Ibid., 4.
63. J. Agada, "Studies of the Personality of Librarians," *Drexel Library Quarterly* 20(2), (1984), 24–45; B. I. Dewey, "Selection of Librarianship as a Career: Implications for Recruitment," *Journal of Education for Librarianship* 26(1), (1985), 16–24; K. M. Heim, *The Status of Women in Librarianship: Historical, Sociological, and Economic Issues* (New York: Neal-Schuman, 1983); R. Kneale, *You Don't Look Like a Librarian: Shattering Stereotypes and Creating Positive New Images in the Internet Age* (Medford, NJ: Information Today, 2009); L. C. Lancaster, "The Click and Clash of Generations," *Library Journal* 128(17), (2003), 36–39; K. Low, *Casanova Was a Librarian: A Light-Hearted Look at the Profession* (Jefferson, NC: McFarland, 2007); Wilson, *Stereotype and Status*.
64. C. A. Julian, "An Analysis of Factors Influencing the Career Choice of Librarianship," in *Special Problems in Librarianship* (Nashville, TN: School of Library Science, George Peabody College for Teachers, 1979), 36; N. A. Van House, "MLS Students' Choice of a Library Career," *Library and Information Science Research* 10(2), (1988), 157–76; R. F. White and D. B. Macklin, *Education, Careers, and Professionalization in Librarianship and Information Science* (Washington, DC: U.S. Office of Education, Bureau of Research, 1970).
65. Portelli, *The Death of Luigi Trastulli;* Thompson, *The Voice of the Past*.
66. P. W. Dalrymple, "Current Trends in Accreditation of LIS Programs," in *Library and Information Studies Education in the United States*, L. Roy and B. E. Sheldon, eds. (London: Mansell, 1998), 81–100.

67. American Library Association, *Standards for Accreditation of Master's Programs in Library and Information Studies,* 2008, www.ala.org/accreditedprograms/sites/ala.org.accreditedprograms/files/content/standards/standards_2008.pdf.
68. Bowker, *Book Industry Statistics* 2008, www.bowker.com/index.php/component/content/article/523.
69. Nora, "Between Memory and History."
70. Crane, "Writing the Individual," 1379.
71. Dale and American Library Association, *A Directory of Oral History Tapes of Librarians.*

Chapter 8

PRACTICAL ORAL HISTORY ADVICE

ORAL HISTORY RESEARCH IS REWARDING WORK. IT IS ALSO SLOW and labor-intensive work. It is rewarding and terribly labor-intensive for the same reason: it builds human relationships.

By its very nature, oral history research builds a bridge between one person and another. The subject tells her story, and the researcher listens. And, frankly, it is hard work to listen. It takes practice to really listen—and not interrupt. It takes practice to listen and gently prod the subject to share more of her own story.

And even if you are video recording the interview—and preserving not only the voice but the gestures and facial animation—you will want to have a very good transcript that can be keyword searchable. You will want something Google-able if you really want to share your work (see the discussion of "lost" oral histories in chapter 7). For your project to endure and be useful, people must be able to find it and access it. It must be described in words that can provide metadata to be included in databases. In the twenty-first century, we let all the words provide the metadata by supplying the entire transcript to a keyword searchable interface: Google. But to take advantage of the search engines, you must have a transcript.

Word-recognition software is becoming better and better; however, nothing can replace the human editor. Each minute of an oral history interview will need careful attention to create a veritable transcript. So even after all the work of securing the recording equipment, finding a quiet recording place, and coordinating the schedules of the subject and the interviewer, there is still much labor-intensive postproduction work to be done for a successful oral history project.

A Story about Human Relationships

Here is a story about how oral history research builds human relationships—and how labor-intensive it is.

As a doctoral student, you first complete your coursework, then you begin thinking about your research project. You might even begin collecting data. But before you can really begin the work, you must pass your qualifying exams (the "writtens" and the "orals") and defend your dissertation proposal. Only after successfully passing your qualifying exams and defending your dissertation proposal are you considered a "doctoral candidate."

My dissertation proposal was ninety-nine pages long and fairly boring. It included an introduction to the theories I planned to test, my research questions, and a very careful and dull plan of action (the "Methods" chapter). The last part of that proposal outlined the major obstacles to completing my project. At that point in the research, I had a corpus of about twelve oral history interviews completed, but only a handful of them had been transcribed. I lamented that the transcription was almost as hard (and took six times as long) as conducting the interview itself.

After I had defended the proposal and celebrated the fact that I was now a doctoral candidate, my mother called to say that she wanted to read the proposal. I warned her that it was a mind-numbing ninety-nine pages, but she insisted. I sent it off to her.

And she must have read the whole thing, because she called a couple of days later to remind me that she had taken professional dictation for many years as a young secretary—including taking dictation for my father—and that she could help with the transcription!

I sent her flash drives with MP3 files of the audio portions of the MP4 video files I had collected, along with a USB foot pedal that controlled the playback on a computer. And she went to work. My mother, Margaret Ann Smith, is almost single-handedly responsible for my finished dissertation through her careful transcription of nearly thirty hour-long interviews.

But here is the human relationship part of the oral history story: Because she spent so much time carefully transcribing those interviews, my mother now intimately knows their stories. As I began the synthesis of the data, she was adamant about how important some of the stories were. Even though she has never met any of the subjects in person, she has an intense relationship with many of them. She still asks me about many of them. My mother particularly remembers Sheila Ross Henderson's stories about the "problem children" and how Ms. Henderson converted them into library patrons. My mother still frequently asks about Sheila.

Oral history work is rewarding and terribly labor-intensive for the same reason: it builds human relationships—with everyone involved.

A Second Story about Human Relationships

I learned how to do oral history from Dr. Martha Norkunas at the University of Texas. She is now at Middle Tennessee State University. At Texas, she was the director of "Interpreting the Texas Past," documenting the history of African Americans in East Austin and particularly the legacy of Jim Crow. In her class we were each assigned to research one aspect of African American life in East Austin, including an oral history interview.

For my project, I chose to research burial practices in East Austin and the mortuaries owned throughout the twentieth century by African Americans. I identified one particular funeral director with whom to conduct the oral history interview because there was so little historical information about his mortuary in the files of the Austin History Center.

I contacted this mortuary and asked if I could interview the funeral director—and he agreed to sit down for two sessions. When I arrived at the mortuary for the first session, I showed him my audio recording equipment and asked where the quietest place might be for an uninterrupted interview. He motioned toward the funeral chapel.

I then told him I would need to set up the digital recorder near an electrical outlet, because the battery probably would not last the full hour. He responded that the only outlet was at the front of the chapel—where a coffin rested on a bier, adorned with flowers. Our interview was to have a silent witness.

(This might sound creepy—and I was a bit anxious about conducting an interview with a stranger, and with another dead stranger within arm's reach—but this silent witness proved to enhance the interview. Several times, when the funeral director was describing his work, and especially how he worked with families to find a burial solution that they could afford, he gestured toward our silent witness and patted the coffin to make a point.)

He was the octogenarian owner of the mortuary, having purchased it late in life after retiring from an illustrious career in administration in Austin's public school system (which he helped to desegregate).

The year was 2008, and during our interview we touched on the momentous and historical possibility of a black man becoming president. At that time in the primaries, the press (and the campaigns) were referring to the candidates as "Obama" and "Hillary." But I noticed that my interview subject physically winced whenever I said the name "Hillary." I assumed that he simply did not like her; however, the wince turned out to be the most profound thing about the oral history interview.

Far from not liking Senator Clinton, my funeral director thought she was the stronger statesman and candidate. He was very anxious to see how the first black candidate was going to fare, but he was actually planning to vote for Hillary in the Texas primary.

This is why oral history is different from journalism or a survey: My subject shared a memory that perfectly and concisely demonstrated the legacy of bigotry, racism, and Jim Crow in the South—and he did this naturally and organically, and almost accidentally.

He was very uncomfortable calling Senator Clinton "Hillary." He explained that when he was a young man, if he had called a white woman by her first name, he would have been lynched.

If I were a journalist with a list of questions, I never could have elicited that response, and a survey certainly would never have collected this datum. But because we were having a discussion—and it was my job to listen carefully and let him tell his own story—he volunteered the memory that caused the physical wince.

This is the legacy of Jim Crow: a well-educated, successful African American man still winces when he hears a white woman referred to by her first name—seventy years later.

Starting a Project

Long before you need to even think about transcribing your work, you will need to collect your interview(s). The following is an annotated checklist of things to consider as you begin an oral history project.

Choose your equipment and your recording format. Every year technology expands and the price of recording equipment becomes lower; however, think carefully about how you ultimately want to disseminate your project when selecting your equipment and recording format. I will not make any recommendations here, because by the time this book is published and in your hands, the options will have probably changed.

What I know is that the recording settings for streaming over the Internet will often not produce a very nice video to be played from a DVD on an HD television. And it is fairly easy to convert a big file into a smaller one, but it is impossible to make a small file a big one. I prefer to record using the highest quality settings I can afford (in both hardware and memory requirements) and then compress the file down to whatever streaming media I want to use. This gives me the option of still publishing the recording on a DVD that will be enjoyable to watch.

Test your recording equipment. Before you sit down with your subject for the first interview, play with your new equipment: record an entire supper, or record yourself making a phone call. And then practice moving the original digital file into the final file types—and examine the results, critically. One thing I failed to grasp early in the project was how small the frame would be displayed within a streaming program on a standard computer monitor. My first video recordings included the entire seated subject—making facial animation very hard to see because that part of the image was ultimately so small when streamed. I learned to focus tightly on the subject's head.

Also, test the entire proposed format migration. Make sure you have all the necessary equipment to turn your original format into the formats that ultimately will be used to disseminate your work. Test the compressions and format migrations on files that you do not care about—you will make mistakes, and it is less stressful if the stakes are low.

Think about the setting. If you use a simple voice recorder, all you need to worry about are the acoustics—but that is plenty to worry about. You will need to position the recording equipment in a way that captures your subject's voice with great clarity and your own voice at least understandably. You will need to find a place not subject to loud outside noises and where you will not be disturbed. Stop and listen quietly in this room before beginning: Is the ceiling fan making a creaking noise? Is there an intercom that could announce a page? If your subject bangs his hand on the desk to make an emphatic point, will that jar the microphone? Does the furniture squeak when you adjust your position? Is it comfortable for a long discussion?

Also, provide your interview subject with a glass of water—you hope she will do a great deal of talking, and you want her to be comfortable.

If you are going to be "filming" the recording (and I understand this is an anachronism in the digital era), you will also need to think about the lighting and the background. Your camera angle will need to be flattering—and finding the most flattering angle can sometimes be challenging.

Think about these factors—and practice finding solutions to these problems—before sitting down with your interview subject, so that you can remain composed and conduct a thoughtful interview.

For your first few interviews, especially if using video equipment, you may want to have a partner—a "best boy" and gaffer—handle the actual recording so you can concentrate on the interview.

Become familiar with your subject. Although the point of oral history is to let the subject tell her or his own story, the interviewer should know something about the subject in order to facilitate a good conversation. In this project, I supplied the volunteer interviewers with some open-ended questions to prompt the discussion if the subject was nervous. "Tell me about a favorite school memory" is a great way to start an interview—it lets your subject begin to focus on a type of memory that we all share and lets the subject set the starting place for the interview. (The interviewee can select an elementary school memory, a high school memory, or a memory from college.)

If you do not share the same age, nationality, or profession of your subject, do some background homework before the interview. Find out where the individual is from and approximately when he was born. Come to the interview knowing a little bit about your subject so that your prompts will have a meaningful reference.

Set the parameters with the subject at the outset. Let your interview subject know what you intend to do with the recording and how long you intend for the recording session to last. You probably will have communicated these things when initially setting up the interview, but it is good to remind the subjects as they are sitting down. A friendly review of your goal will suffice—for example, "Your children have asked me to record this oral history interview with you. We'll have about one hour before the tape begins to run out on this recorder."

Letting the subjects know your expectations for the interview's length can help them to pace their story. And it will give you a designated time to ask, "We have five minutes left—do you have any final thoughts or advice?"

Have an opening statement prepared. If you are doing a series of interviews for a themed project, have an opening script prepared to introduce each interview. State the date and the place where the interview is being recorded. Introduce your subject with the salient details that will help frame the interview.

If the interview is for an institution, your opening statement should include who will "own" the recording and what it may be used for. That institution's legal department may want to vet this language. If you are working with a university, your Institutional Review Board (IRB) may want you to include certain specific informed-consent language.

Conduct a final practice interview using your equipment with a friend. Now that you have mastered using the equipment and formatting your files, have a real beta test with a trusted friend. Use the opening statement you have crafted, and see how it sounds on the finished recording—you may be surprised how difficult it can be to rattle off even a prepared statement. This is your opportunity to practice.

If possible, sit down in the proposed recording space and record a conversation—where you practice listening and only prompting your subject friend to explore his memories. But if your proposed recording space for your first real interview is not available, practice in a space that is not ideal so that you can see and hear exactly how irritating certain disruptions can be to the recording process.

Begin your interview with an open-ended question that can frame the entire interview. One way I like to begin life story interviews is to ask the narrators to describe their birth certificate—in as much detail as they are comfortable with. What year (or decade) were they born? Where? What is their name on the certificate? What are their parents' names on the certificate?

A Final Meditation on Oral History

For all the theory that I have learned, and all the variations of methodology that I have practiced, the truth is that the production of a good oral history is almost non-scholarly. (The scholarship is really about how I have used the oral history interview, how I have interpreted the corpus of interviews.) Good oral history is the result of two people's patience and generosity.

The narrator must come to the table willing to share—or at least be willing to be willing to share—her memories, her fears, and her wisdom.

The interviewer must come to the table with an open mind—and heart—to listen and let the narrator tell *her* story. And both participants must have already done a great deal of planning and footwork to make the meeting happen. The interviewer must also be committed to following through with the project so that the narrator's story—and time—is not wasted by becoming a forgotten recording with no way for posterity to access it.

Both parties must be vulnerable. The interviewer must be able to set aside all of his expectations and find a way to make the subject comfortable enough to begin to share her story. For me, this meant disarming myself of my usual rhetorical weapons. (These include the yearning to "win the argument," to prove I'm the smartest person in the room, to have the last word.) In order to capture my subject's story, I have to come to the table as her servant.

For a good oral history, the narrator must trust the interviewer to be her servant and the steward of her memories. The best oral histories are not simple recitations of the "facts" of someone's life, but a thoughtful recollection of her feelings and fears while making the decisions that shaped her life. Vulnerability is implicit anytime we talk about fears and feelings.

I encourage you to use this methodology to document the stories of the people who are important to you. It is a beautiful gift to give a treasured family member, colleague, or friend. It is a beautiful way to become connected to someone you admire. It will make you a better person—and preserve what you admire about your subject.

Bibliography

ACT UP. *ACT UP (AIDS Coalition to Unleash Power) Oral History Project.* Available from www.actuporalhistory.org/.

Agada, J. 1984. "Studies of the Personality of Librarians." *Drexel Library Quarterly* 20 (2): 24–45.

American Library Association. 2010. *Standards for Accreditation of Master's Programs in Library and Information Studies, 2008.* Available from www.ala.org/accreditedprograms/sites/ala.org.accreditedprograms/files/content/standards/standards_2008.pdf.

American Library Association. Office for Intellectual Freedom. 2010. *Intellectual Freedom Manual.* 8th ed. Chicago: American Library Association.

Arsenault, Raymond. 2006. *Freedom Riders: 1961 and the Struggle for Racial Justice.* Pivotal Moments in American History. New York: Oxford University Press.

Bowker. *Book Industry Statistics 2008.* Available from www.bowker.com/index.php/component/content/article/523.

Brown, Cynthia Stokes. 1988. *Like It Was: A Complete Guide to Writing Oral History.* New York: Teachers and Writers Collaborative.

Campos, David. 2006. "Slave Narratives from the Federal Writers' Project 1936–1938: Stories as a Catalyst for Historical Comprehension." *Black History Bulletin* 69 (2): 8–14.

Capra, Frank, James Stewart, Donna Reed, Lionel Barrymore, Frances Goodrich, and Albert Hackett. 1946. *It's a Wonderful Life.* Australia: Bounty. Videorecording.

Confino, A. 1997. "Collective Memory and Cultural History: Problems of Method." *American Historical Review* 102 (5): 1386–1403.

Connerton, Paul. 1989. *How Societies Remember: Themes in the Social Sciences.* Cambridge and New York: Cambridge University Press.

Coser, Lewis A. 1992. "Introduction." In *On Collective Memory,* edited by M. Halbwachs and L. A. Coser. Chicago: University of Chicago Press.

Crane, Susan A. 1997. "Writing the Individual Back into Collective Memory." *American Historical Review* 102 (5): 1372–85.

Cukor, George, Franz Waxman, Cary Grant, Katharine Hepburn, James Stewart, Ruth Hussey, John Howard, Roland Young, John Halliday, Mary Nash, Virginia Weidler, Joseph L. Mankiewicz, Philip Barry, Metro-Goldwyn-Mayer, Turner Entertainment Co., and Warner Home Video (Firm). 2000 [1940]. *The Philadelphia Story.* Burbank, CA: Turner Entertainment, Warner Home Video. Videorecording.

Daily, Jay E., and Eugene R. Hanson. 2009. "Catalogs and Cataloging: History." In *Encyclopedia of Library and Information Sciences.* 3rd ed. New York: Taylor and Francis.

Dale, Doris Cruger, and American Library Association. 1986. *A Directory of Oral History Tapes of Librarians in the United States and Canada.* Chicago: American Library Association.

Dalrymple, Prudence W. 1998. "Current Trends in Accreditation of LIS Programs." In *Library and Information Studies Education in the United States,* edited by L. Roy and B. E. Sheldon. London; Washington, DC: Mansell.

DeBlasio, Donna Marie. 2009. *Catching Stories: A Practical Guide to Oral History.* Athens, OH: Swallow Press.

Dewey, B. I. 1985. "Selection of Librarianship as a Career: Implications for Recruitment." *Journal of Education for Librarianship* 26 (1): 16–24.

Frisch, Michael H. 1990. *A Shared Authority: Essays on the Craft and Meaning of Oral and Public History*. SUNY Series in Oral and Public History. Albany: State University of New York Press.

———. 2006. "Oral History and the Digital Revolution: Toward a Post-Documentary Sensibility." In *The Oral History Reader*, edited by R. Perks and A. Thomson. New York: Routledge.

Govenar, Alan B. 2000. *African American Frontiers: Slave Narratives and Oral Histories*. Santa Barbara, CA: ABC-CLIO.

Green, Anna. 2004. "Individual Remembering and 'Collective Memory': Theoretical Presuppositions and Contemporary Debates." *Oral History* 32 (2): 35–44.

Grimes, Deborah J. 1994. "Marian the Librarian—The Truth behind the Image." In *Discovering Librarians: Profiles of a Profession*, edited by M. J. Scherdin. Chicago: Association of College and Research Libraries, American Library Association.

Halbwachs, Maurice. 1980. *The Collective Memory*. New York: Harper and Row.

———. 1992. *On Collective Memory*. Chicago: University of Chicago Press.

Hampton, Henry, Steve Fayer, and Sarah Flynn. 1990. *Voices of Freedom: An Oral History of the Civil Rights Movement from the 1950s through the 1980s*. New York: Bantam Books.

Heim, Kathleen M. 1983. *The Status of Women in Librarianship: Historical, Sociological, and Economic Issues*. New York: Neal-Schuman.

Julian, C. A. 1979. "An Analysis of Factors Influencing the Career Choice of Librarianship." In *Special Problems in Librarianship*. Nashville, TN: School of Library Science, George Peabody College for Teachers.

Kirkland, Jessica, A. Arro Smith, and Loriene Roy. 2010. "Capturing Our Stories and GLIFOS: Rich-Media Video." *Electronic Library* 28 (5): 650–56.

Kneale, Ruth. 2009. *You Don't Look Like a Librarian: Shattering Stereotypes and Creating Positive New Images in the Internet Age*. Medford, NJ: Information Today.

Lancaster, L. C. 2003. "The Click and Clash of Generations." *Library Journal* 128 (17): 36–39.

Landman, Janet. 1993. *Regret: The Persistence of the Possible*. New York: Oxford University Press.

Lang, Walter, William Marchant, Henry Ephron, Phoebe Ephron, Leon Shamroy, Cyril J. Mockridge, Katharine Hepburn, Spencer Tracy, Gig Young, and Joan Blondell. 2004 [1957]. *Desk Set*. Beverly Hills, CA: CBS/Fox Video. Videorecording.

Library of Congress, Veterans History Project. *Veterans History Project Collection (Library of Congress), circa 1914–2007*. Available from www.loc.gov/vets/vets-home.html.

Low, Kathleen. 2007. *Casanova Was a Librarian: A Light-Hearted Look at the Profession*. Jefferson, NC: McFarland.

Nora, Pierre. 1989. "Between Memory and History: Les Lieux de Mémoire." *Representations* (26): 7–24.

Olick, Jeffrey K., and Joyce Robbins. 1998. "Social Memory Studies: From 'Collective Memory' to the Historical Sociology of Mnemonic Practices." *Annual Review of Sociology* 24 (1): 105–40.

"Oral History of the [U.S.] House [of Representatives]." Available from http://oralhistory.clerk.house.gov.

Perks, Robert, and Alistair Thomson. 2006. "Critical Developments: Introduction." In *The Oral History Reader*, edited by R. Perks and A. Thomson. New York: Routledge.

Portelli, Alessandro. 1991. *The Death of Luigi Trastulli, and Other Stories: Form and Meaning in Oral History*. SUNY Series in Oral and Public History. Albany: State University of New York Press.

———. 2003. *The Order Has Been Carried Out: History, Memory, and Meaning of a Nazi Massacre in Rome*. New York: Palgrave Macmillan.

Popular Memory Group. 2006. "Popular Memory: Theory, Politics, Method." In *The Oral History Reader,* edited by R. Perks and A. Thomson. New York: Routledge.

Rosaldo, R. 1989. "Imperialist Nostalgia." *Representations* 26: 107–22.

Sharpless, Rebecca. 2008. "The History of Oral History." In *Handbook of Oral History,* edited by T. L. Charlton, L. E. Myers, and R. Sharpless. Lanham, MD: AltaMira Press.

Shaw, Nate, and Theodore Rosengarten. 2000. *All God's Dangers: The Life of Nate Shaw.* Chicago: University of Chicago Press.

Sitton, Thad, George L. Mehaffy, and O. L. Davis. 1983. *Oral History: A Guide for Teachers (and Others.* Austin: University of Texas Press.

Smith, A. Arro. 2006. "Internet Filtering Policy and Attitudes in Texas Public Libraries." *Texas Library Journal* 82 (4): 148–51.

———. 2008. "Cataloging Heresy." In *Radical Cataloging: Essays at the Front,* edited by K. R. Roberto. Jefferson, NC: McFarland.

———. 2013. *"Capturing Our Stories" Oral Histories Program, 2005-2012 97/1/70.* American Library Association Archives at the University of Illinois at Urbana-Champaign. Available from http://archives.library.illinois.edu/alaarchon/?p=collections/controlcard&id=8511.

Smith, A. Arro, and Loriene Roy. 2009. *Capturing Our Stories: Developing a National Oral History Program of Retiring/Retired Librarians.* Available from www.ischool.utexas.edu/~stories/.

Smith, Linda Tuhiwai. 1999. *Decolonizing Methodologies: Research and Indigenous Peoples.* London: Zed Books.

Sommer, Barbara W., and Mary Kay Quinlan. 2009. *The Oral History Manual.* 2nd ed. American Association for State and Local History Book Series. Lanham, MD: AltaMira Press.

StoryCorps. *StoryCorps Collection.* Available from www.storycorps.net.

Terkel, Studs. 1970. *Hard Times: An Oral History of the Great Depression.* New York: Pantheon Books.

———. 1974. *Working: People Talk about What They Do All Day and How They Feel about What They Do.* New York: Pantheon Books.

Thompson, Paul Richard. 2000. *The Voice of the Past: Oral History.* 3rd ed. Oxford, England and New York: Oxford University Press.

Tisdale, John R. 2000. "Observational Reporting as Oral History: How Journalists Interpreted the Death and Destruction of Hurricane Audrey." *Oral History Review* 27 (2): 41–65.

Van House, N. A. 1988. "MLS Students' Choice of a Library Career." *Library and Information Science Research* 10 (2): 157–76.

Vansina, J. 1985. *Oral Tradition as History.* London: James Currey.

Wessells, Michael. 2000. "I Faced Dr. Laura—and Survived!" *American Libraries* 31 (10): 56.

White, Rodney F., and David B. Macklin. 1970. *Education, Careers, and Professionalization in Librarianship and Information Science.* Washington, DC: U.S. Office of Education, Bureau of Research.

Wigginton, Eliot. 1972. *The Foxfire Book: Hog Dressing; Log Cabin Building; Mountain Crafts and Foods; Planting by the Signs; Snake Lore, Hunting Tales, Faith Healing; Moonshining; and Other Affairs of Plain Living.* Garden City, NY: Doubleday.

Wilson, Pauline. 1982. *Stereotype and Status: Librarians in the United States.* Contributions in Librarianship and Information Science. Westport, CT: Greenwood Press.

Works Progress Administration and Federal Writers' Project. 2010. *Portraits of African American Ex-Slaves from the U.S. Works Progress Administration, Federal Writers' Project Slave Narratives Collections.* Available from http://memory.loc.gov/ammem/snhtml/snhome.html.

X, Malcolm, and Alex Haley. 1965. *The Autobiography of Malcolm X.* New York: Grove Press.

Young, Robert. 2003. *Postcolonialism: A Very Short Introduction.* New York: Oxford University Press.

Index

Y